AF574026

YUP THE ORGANIZATION

JAMES E.
WAVADA

Yup the Organization

HOW TO $UCCEED IN BUSINESS WITH SAVVY, SMARTS, AND STYLE

JAMES E. WAVADA

FRANKLIN WATTS
New York Toronto
1986

Library of Congress Cataloging-in-Publication Data

Wavada, James E.
Yup the organization.

Includes index.
1. Success in business. I. Title.
HF5386.W247 1986 650.1'4 85-22799
ISBN 0-531-15503-X

6 5 4 3 2 1

CONTENTS

YUP THE ORGANIZATION

To Dolores—
Whose encouragement
("Of course you can do it.")
and understanding all the
while it was being written
made this book possible.

PREFACE

From the early days of our youth our ears are filled with exhortations to achieve. Parents, aunts, uncles, grandparents, teachers, professors, counselors, preachers, priests, and rabbis urge us to study diligently; earn high grades; achieve as many degrees as possible; set high goals; excel at every endeavor; hustle; move to the top; and understand that "Winning isn't everything—it is the only thing."

Whether reaching the top in the business world truly deserves to be life's highest goal is left to the sociologists, theologians, and psychologists to debate. This book concerns itself solely with providing you the easiest ways of getting to the top, should getting there be your goal.

You may be asking yourself: "What? Another book on how to reach the executive suite? Who needs it?" Admittedly, tons of tomes have been written and millions of words have been spoken on how to succeed in business. But, sad to say, far too little information has been provided on how to develop to full potential the most important single quality needed for advancing in the business world—acting ability.

Why is acting ability so vital? The reason is found in the word which practically all business leaders cite as the single most important criterion of advancement—*performance. Webster's New Collegiate Dictionary* offers a number of definitions of "performance." Concentrate on these two, "the action of representing a character in a play; a public presentation or exhibition." Turning in a good performance, as described in these definitions, will get you where you want to go in the business world.

This book resulted from a firm conviction, based on long experience in and close observation of the business world, that if actual results were really the major considerations in selecting people for promotion, each business would display in a prominent place scoreboards showing the final consequences of each executive decision. If such a practice were followed, advancement policies would be simple and clear cut. Those with the highest totals would move up; those with the lowest would move out. But, alas, there are no scoreboards in business, only performance appraisal forms in abundance, which are usually completed on the basis of impressions, perceptions, and subjective judgments.

Another conviction brought this book into being: There isn't nearly as much difference in the actual abilities of those at the top and those in middle management as there is in the perception of their skills. The really big difference between those at the top and those in the middle is in the amount of pay and perks received.

This book depicts the show known as American business, not as serious drama or as tragedy, but rather as comedy. As Jonathan Swift wrote: "Satire is a sort of glass, wherein beholders do generally discover everybody's face but their own."

Is the foregoing to be construed as indicating that the American business system is evil, deceptive, or even worse? Of course not. Its record over the past two hundred plus years proves beyond a doubt that, warts and all, it is by far the best system in being.

Is this book an indictment of the people who run American business as evil, deceptive, or even worse? Of course not. Rather, it urges you, and shows you how, to be as smart as they are.

It is said that participants in poker games laugh and tell jokes when they are winning and shout "Deal the cards" when they are losing. This book is actually a case of a beneficiary of the American business system laughing and telling jokes about something which has been very good to him. It is written in the hope of bringing enjoyment to readers who "discover everybody's face but their own."

CHAPTER 1

BECOME A DEDICATED ROLE PLAYER

To be truly effective, role playing must be a constant, rather than occasional, activity. To capitalize fully on the big edge in career advancement highly skilled role playing offers, you must be thoroughly convinced of the power of role playing and firmly dedicated to learning and doing what is required to become a stellar role player. In the words of a great philosopher: ''You gotta believe.''

To understand why role playing offers an easier and shorter road to the top, look around you. Observe those pulling in the big bucks, enjoying the fancy perks, and flouting their power. See how they concentrate on making the proper impressions and creating the appropriate effects. They play a role.

Turn your attention now to the non-role players in your show—the doers. Watch them working their hearts out and living off the leftovers. They perform a function.

First, then, accept the fact that how able one *appears* to be counts for more than how able one actually *is.* Base your every action on the unfailing truth of business life that appearance always triumphs over reality.

Second, understand that top role-playing skills can be acquired; one doesn't have to be born with them. Born role players do begin with an advantage, but careful study of the role-playing art and strong determination to become a good actor can quickly close the gap. Also recognize that role playing is not limited to those just beginning business careers. Even faithful servant-types who have done their jobs and stayed in the background with very little to show for their dedicated efforts, can spruce up their acts considerably. It is said of spiritual salvation that it is never too late to change one's ways. So, too, it is never too late to become a dedicated role player.

Nor is role playing limited strictly to men. Of course, men still dominate business executive suites, and through long participation in the art are master role players. But the role of women in business has shifted significantly in the past two decades, and the pace of that change should accelerate in the future. All but the crustiest of curmudgeons have come to recognize that women have brains as well as bodies and are able to play leading roles in business.

Women in business are presently being bombarded with advice, most of it conflicting, on how to move up the corporate ladder. Wise ones will use the method employed successfully by past and present business leaders—role playing—and beat them at their own game.

It would be wonderful to say that now, at long last, women in business are judged solely on ability and have exactly the same opportunities as men. But it would be untrue. For a few still judge women according to their willingness to perform in the bedroom. Others piously declare that women should not be paid the same amount as men doing the same type of work because "their husbands have good jobs" or "they are not raising families." And there are some who give women high-sounding titles and reasonably good salaries so they can play the role of mannequin to be placed in a display window to placate the EEOC, Affirmative Action, and NOW people.

In today's world a woman shouldn't put up with such nonsense. Rather, she should develop and use her role-playing skills to become a top executive.

But understand, too, that role playing is not for everyone. At least average intelligence and management skills, plus a strong desire to move to the top are required to put on an attention-getting act. You must have a pretty good idea of what you are doing to appear as if you really know what you are doing.

Always, role players are realists, recognizing the folly of believing that doing a good job and staying in the background will produce ample rewards. They accept the fact that getting ahead in business demands thinking of themselves first and taking each action or speaking each word on the basis of what is most likely to impress the powers that be. But they are not con people. Sooner or later con people get caught. Good role players don't.

Role playing is certainly not a new development. Role players probably existed in the Stone Age. Those founders of the art lived in the biggest caves and carried the biggest clubs.

Over the centuries role playing has evolved into a more refined and exacting art. History books are full of examples of cunning characters who cozened kings and princes, and also some queens and princesses, into providing them sinecures. With the coming of the Industrial Revolution the pace of role playing picked up sharply. The wise players quickly concluded it was much more comfortable and profitable to sit in an office than to stand behind a machine or be a cog in an assembly line. The Depression of the 1930s transformed role playing from an art providing profit and comfort into the most effective means of survival.

TV's invasion of the home enabled the role-playing art to take a quantum leap forward. Through the tube even the common folk became aware of the importance of appearance in making favorable impressions. How well one dressed, spoke, and conducted oneself determined how well one was accepted. No wonder, then, that so many top role players now use TV to practice and polish their acts.

Role playing has not been problem free. Watergate dealt the art a damaging blow. As a phalanx of well-groomed, poised, well-spoken government officials, oozing couth from every pore, paraded before the TV cameras, a pattern emerged quickly and clearly. These bright young men were not what they appeared to be. Their sworn testimony, subsequent events proved, bore little, if any, resemblance to the actual facts. They committed the capital sin of role playing. They got caught in their acts.

As soon as the lid blew off Watergate, the media began to describe these poised and articulate men as plastic people—an act not without irony, since the media include some of the world's greatest role players. Moralizers in academe ranted against the Watergaters' vulgar display of duplicity and deceit. Preachers thundered against the immorality of it all.

Vietnam also put a temporary crimp in role playing. College kids, dropouts, hippies, and flower children, fairly bursting with the largess of their role-playing parents, took to the streets to bring justice, peace, and truth to the world through marching, singing, reefer puffing, rioting, and general peevishness. Smashing the icons of their elders was their goal. Their aim was faulty. The icons survived and the kids eventually got haircuts, bathed, and went to work. In fact, some of these former rowdies are now outstanding role players.

With the oil embargo imposed by the Arab states in 1973, the ensuing recession, and high rates of inflation previously regarded as unthinkable, came the rekindling of the light. Americans regained their senses. Moralisms which emerged with Watergate and Vietnam were discarded. The deep recession which began in 1980 and even reached into the executive ranks, demonstrated clearly that people had better get their acts together unless they wanted to end up walking the streets.

President Reagan's openly expressed fervent admiration for Calvin Coolidge prompted all true believers to rejoin the ranks by expressing adherence to Cal's philosophy of "The business of America is business.'' Role playing thrives now as never before.

''Play your cards right'' is a cliché frequently employed when advising someone on how to succeed. ''Play your role to perfection'' is much more apt, for in these five words lie the proven means of achieving greater power, status, pay, and perks.

Far too many people in the business world today face their futures in much the same way A. E. Housman described life in *Last Poems:*

And how am I to face the odds
of man's bedevilment and God's?
I, a stranger and afraid
in a world I never made.

In business all of the bedevilment comes from man. God doesn't get involved. But any bedevilment encountered can be coped with successfully by speaking every word and taking every action on the basis of making the best possible impression.

Role playing may not, probably won't, make your world precisely the way you want it to be. But it will certainly make it a hell of a lot better.

If you are now fully committed to becoming an accomplished role player, read on. Following the instructions given in the pages of this book, and referring to them as particular situations arise, will enable you to develop into a stellar performer.

CHAPTER 2

GET YOUR ACT TOGETHER

What you are is pretty much established by now. It's never too late, however, to improve the way you project yourself. Keep in mind that what you project yourself to be closely parallels what you are perceived to be by the people who decide your fate.

As you begin to put your act together, observe a prime prerequisite of effective role playing—you must appear to be a good performer before you will be given the opportunity to perform. Anyone appearing to be a klutz never is given a chance to perform.

YOUR NAME

What can you do at this point about making your name more appealing? A lot more than you probably think.

If you are among the unfortunates bearing the heavy burden of a nickname hung on you in your youth—Sis, Peaches, Twinky, Bud, Butch, Buster, Shorty, or the like—

drop it at once. None of these monikers bespeaks star quality.

Many nicknames derived from given first names are also taboo. John may use Jack, but never Johnny. James should use neither James nor Jimmy, only Jim. Kenneth is acceptable, Ken much better, and Kenny totally unthinkable. Robert is OK, Bob much better, and Rob a bit too preppy. William is acceptable, Bill better, and Will or Willie strictly forbidden.

Mary-something names—Mary Lou, Mary Ann—are OK in school but not in business. Become Mary. In fact all double names—Judith Ann, Emma Jane, and the like—should be discarded. Women are well advised to use actual first names rather than nicknames—Katherine instead of Kate, Dorothy rather than Dot, Patricia, not Pat. But it must be recognized that a woman named Geraldine who goes by Gerry became well known. A Mary Kay has also done quite well in business.

First names which are also surnames can be decided assets. Taylor, Porter, Palmer, Nelson, Hamilton, and so forth sound quite old family, a characteristic highly respected in the executive suite.

Surnames as middle names are even more common. If that name enjoys, or once enjoyed, prominence in the community, it should certainly be used. Anyone named Gustavus (in honor of his paternal grandfather) Reeves (out of respect to his mother's family, which at one time was prominent in the community) is well advised to use G. Reeves. In addition to being easier to pronounce, Reeves sounds more socially acceptable.

Roman numeral III following the surname is always impressive, as it conveys good breeding and family tradition. All men should check the possibilities of being a III. A grandfather and uncle may have the same first and middle names as you. If so, add III, at least for business purposes. II is almost as impressive.

Some women are now retaining their family name after marriage. Others use their family name as if it were a middle name, while others keep it as part of a hyphenated last name: Mary Brown marries Bill Black and becomes Mary

Brown-Black. Women who keep their family name in some manner flash the signal they are independent and intend to accomplish something besides just cleaning house and raising kids. Women seeking to get ahead in business are wise to retain their family name in the manner with which they are most comfortable.

Anyone so unfortunate as to be stuck with an unusual first name, such as Matilda, Hortense, Gisela, Willadean, Myrtle, Alphonse, Ignatius, Lorenzo, Sylvester, or Cornelius should use the first initial of her or his first name and full middle name—providing the middle name isn't worse.

Even strange-sounding first or middle names are better than initials. There was a time when business tycoons were known by initials such as B J or T R, but the practice is vanishing even in the South and Southwest where it once flourished (in real life as well as popular TV shows). Using both first and middle names, such as Billy Joe or Jimmy Ray, is fine for a man aspiring to be a country-and-western singer.

Although not much, if anything, can be done to add to the appeal of a surname, aspiring role players should at least be aware of its importance to their acts. Black is black, brown is brown, and yellow is yellow. White has many shades.

One-syllable surnames are most favored, two-syllable ones quite acceptable. Hyphenated last names, such as Smythe-Browne, are especially impressive. Having a name which sounds "very American" offers quite an advantage. That it is easy to pronounce and remember is also useful. Leaders don't like to make mistakes. If the leading players aren't certain how to correctly pronounce a last name, chances are good they won't call it.

Anyone with a name somewhat difficult to spell or pronounce knows from experience to expect the question: "What nationality are you?" In such situations, give the country of origin of your surname, and if that represents half or less of your ethnic composition, mention the other components of your nationality. But use common sense. Don't go into turgid detail such as "my mother's maiden name was Cox, her mother's Irwin, my father's Churchill, and my father's paternal grandmother's Gordon." Such a detailed explanation will likely bring a look of ". . doth protest too much methinks" to the inquirer's face. If your last name is "very American" sounding, never volunteer that your mother's maiden name was Pastoriti, her mother's Cryzkanski, and your father's mother's Wasserstein.

Only after you have become thoroughly convinced that your last name places a serious obstacle in your career path should you consider changing it. Discarding the family name will surely bring a waterfall of tears to your parents' eyes, probably to your aunts' and uncles', and certainly to your grandparents'. Your friends will be very amused. Special complications will arise if you have children. Follow your convictions by taking a leaf from the book of many show business stars. Change your name to one easily pronounced and remembered. A Stanislaus Joseph Perchiamski or Edythe Opal Koppolous would be difficult, if not impossible, to find in an executive suite. A Stanley J. Perch or Edith O. Kopp would fit quite nicely.

EDUCATION

Where you went to school is as important, sometimes more so, than what you studied or how much smarts you acquired. Your parents spent a lot of money getting you a degree. Make the most of it. The more prestigious the school you attended, the more you can make out of it.

Graduates of fancy institutions are usually especially highly regarded in the hinterlands. Heads of some lower profile companies treat grads of the prestigious schools as trophies to be displayed to prove that the Fortune 500s don't have a monopoly on top talent.

But in educational background, as in all other facets of getting to the top, there are no absolutes. One must always anticipate what's in and what's out at each particular company. Holders of degrees from elite centers of learning may face two particular problems:

1. Attendance at such schools reeks of silver spoonism. Suspicions will arise that the grad joined the company

through family connections with the big boss, hereafter referred to in this book as CEO. Number two who covets the top spot may become quite concerned, especially if he or she is a graduate of a school not dripping with distinction.

2. CEOs with degrees earned through fourteen years of both summers and winters at night schools are not awed by graduates of fancy schools. That all but extinct breed of CEOs without a degree from a college or university frequently is motivated to hire those from hot-shot institutions solely for the great pleasure derived from firing them.

Holders of degrees from hotsy-totsy schools confronted with either of these two situations must downplay their academic backgrounds. Anyone in this fix who holds another degree from a less fancy institution may relieve the pressure to some extent by emphasizing attendance at the lesser place and not talking about the one which raises the hackles of the hierarchy.

Regardless of whether it is or isn't advantageous to brag about the elite learning place you attended, close contact should be maintained with the school and its local alumni chapter. Keep the ties bound on a sub rosa basis if you must, but do it. Membership in the local club of a fancy school puts you in close contact with those who can give you a more important position in a good company.

Constantly looking for key contacts who can accelerate your pace of progress is an important factor in getting ahead. Polishing this act should be an ongoing activity.

If neither situation applies, emphasize your school affiliation as much as reasonably good taste permits. If you hold a graduate degree from a school fancier than the one from which you received your undergraduate degree, say a lot about the former and very little about the latter.

State universities are acceptable, with some more acceptable than others. Graduates of New Jersey's state university, Rutgers, have a special advantage. Rutgers sounds much fancier than "The University of Such-and-Such a State."

Universities with State in their official name are still associated primarily with the agricultural field. Most colleges and universities bearing the name of a city are not impressive. Small denominational liberal arts schools are considered better only than not having attended any institution of higher learning. Branches of state universities, with one or two exceptions, are equally devoid of status. If you attended one, mention the university but don't mention the campus site.

If you are a fraternity man, always wear your ring and refer frequently to prominent fraternity brothers. You may be so fortunate as to be a member of the fraternity to which your CEO belongs. If so, make the most of this fortunate coincidence by trying to become president of your local chapter to impress him with your leadership qualities.

If you belong to a sorority, let your membership be known to everyone you need to impress. It is less likely that sorority sisterhood will produce immediate benefits, since men still dominate the executive suite. But it can help in the future and it certainly won't hurt you if CEO's wife is a sorority sister. But your sorority affiliation must be with an institution of higher learning. So-called "Social Sororities" are a negative—members of the steno pool can belong to them.

Should you have been so imprudent, some may say impudent, not to have joined a fraternity or sorority, keep it to yourself. Don't apologize for not being a frat boy or sorority girl. Rather, follow the advice of Henry Ford II: "Never complain, never explain."

Academic accomplishments may be detailed, but never flaunted. Phi Beta Kappa keys may be displayed decorously. Membership in MENSA is allowed, but a big deal should not be made of it.

Men who played a varsity sport in college usually are wise to downplay their jock past, at least until they have become firmly established as a comer. Being hung with the label "dumb jock" can be quite damaging. For some reason no athlete is referred to as a "smart jock," not even a Bill Bradley, a Rhodes Scholar and United States Senator. As male jocks move up to better jobs, it is not only permissible, but also advisable for them to publicize their athletic feats. Inexplicably, several former third-stringers have evolved into ex-All-Americans since becoming CEOs.

A man may emphasize his athletic background if he was recruited because of the publicity his jock feats generated, or if he was a star at the school CEO attended. All former jocks should concentrate on developing role-playing skills. Yesterday's heroes are quickly forgotten.

Women should not refer to athletic accomplishments in school for, unfortunately, athletics is one of a number of areas in which business applies a double standard. But being an above-average tennis player or golfer can be a plus. Former cheer leaders are also well advised to stay silent about their rah-rah days.

RELIGION

As a general rule, the less said about religion, the better. Those who wear their religion on their sleeves frequently get their arms caught in the wringer.

Even in this so-called age of enlightened tolerance the words "atheist" and "agnostic" fall heavily upon the ears. People in either category should never identify themselves as such, but rather as people who live by the Golden Rule instead of by regulations of institutionalized churches. Only unreconstructed bigots can find fault with the Golden Rule.

FAMILY BACKGROUND

Much caution is called for here. As a general rule, the less said about roots, the better.

If your father, grandfather, or another relative organized or now controls the company, everyone knows it and acts accordingly. Enough resentment about your presence presently exists without your calling more attention to your bloodlines.

If you obtained your position through a family friendship with top management, be smart enough to keep quiet about it. The office grapevine will spread the word quickly enough. Involved here is an essential ingredient of top-flight role playing—using the help of others to obtain better parts, while making it appear you did it entirely on your own. Work hard to create the fiction you were picked because of your outstanding performance record in your previous work.

If your father is, or was, a blue-collar worker, the leading lights may question your social mobility and capacity to interact effectively with higher-ups, should your beginnings become common knowledge. Not only must a role player interact effectively, he must also use quite frequently the word "interact." Calling your father "plant superintendent" may be the best solution.

Make no reference to a deceased father's occupation unless he was at least an assistant vice president. If he died within the last several years, don't mention his business connection unless he was a vice president or higher. Refer to your mother only if she held a management position in business or was a professional of some type.

Successful brothers or sisters can be assets. Should you have one who is making good, spread the word to your superiors to impress them with the high quality of your bloodlines. Success in the business world is best, athletics acceptable (only tennis or golf for sisters), academe nothing to shout about, and the field of entertainment strictly taboo.

Word that you are a cousin, nephew, or niece of a leading light will spread quickly throughout the office, even if you have a different surname. Brush off any significance of the relationship with the comment: "He goes his way and I go mine." No one will laugh, but some will find it difficult to suppress a snicker.

Members of once wealthy families that subsequently lost the family jewels are wise not to identify themselves with the folks who failed. Being tagged a loser is not an asset. When confronted with the facts, refer to the relationship as a shirttail one.

A man who married into a family loaded with money, known officially as "affluent," should keep quiet about it if his wife's family played any part in getting him his position. If in-laws used no influence, he should spread the word of his connection to the money pipeline as subtly, but as widely, as he can, especially among the leading players. Marrying money demonstrates possession of at least one special skill. Mogul fathers-in-law should be introduced at least to immediate bosses, and higher-ups too, if possible. Rich mothers-in-law should be kept at home.

Marrying well is another area in which women must use an act different from men. Say nothing about your private passageway to the vault. And make sure hubby doesn't play the role of Little Lord Fauntleroy around your business associates. Don't display either fat cat mother-in-law or father-in-law at your office. The boys you passed up will spread the word with comments such as: "I knew there was some catch. No woman can make it on her own."

PREVIOUS EXPERIENCE

Regardless of why you left your previous company, your assignment is to convince one and all you were picked for your present post because of your spectacular performance. And stick with your story. If you were selected by a head hunter, known officially as an "executive recruiter," spread the word, making sure everyone understands you were picked from a slew of candidates. You begin with more status than does someone who walked in off the street.

Be prepared to answer numerous questions about your previous business connections. Queries from "lifers" will be especially sharp. Instinctively, "lifers" question the moral fiber of anyone changing jobs.

Implicit in the questions will be: "If XYZ is such a great company, and you are such a hotshot, why in the hell did you come to this place?" Generalize as much as you can, but never reply: "For more money." Already your new associates are overwhelmed with curiosity about your salary. Don't encourage them to learn the amount. If they want to know, they can and will find a way. Even small offices have at least one individual who knows all the inside information. If your pay is less than lavish you will receive no respect. If you are earning more than most of your peers you will immediately become their prime target. No need to hurry that happening. It will occur soon enough. The more time you have to prepare your defense against attacks from peers, the more effective it should be.

If you were fired, now referred to officially as "outplaced," never admit it. *Never!* Even using such terms as "by mutual agreement" will mark you as a cripple.

Avoid knocking former bosses. Even incompetent, dishonest, or tyrannical bastards should be praised. To be critical might scar you from the start as not a team player, a very black mark indeed.

If you owned all or part of a business which went broke or were a leading light in a company suffering the same fate, keep quiet about it. If some smart aleck asks questions, tell him the business was sold or that you had been planning for some time to make a change.

Say what you want to about previous associations free of fear of being contradicted by leading players at your former company. With all the government regulations covering employment practices, all businesses are now afraid to tell the truth. At least, they should be.

Previous experience in sales should always be referred to as "marketing." If travel was involved, talk about it only if you did it all by airplane. Covering a territory by car is a decided negative.

SOCIAL STANDING

Demonstrating to the top executives in your company that both you and your spouse are quite able and very willing to mix with and impress the local gentry is essential in being regarded as potential top management material.

To attract favorable attention in the social scene you must, absolutely must, belong to a club. The kind of club you should belong to depends upon where you live. If you are in a very large metropolitan area you will need to belong to at least one fancy dining club. But many players in big cities believe it also necessary to belong to a prestigious country club, even if they do not play tennis or golf. Those who live in the suburbs of large cities or mid-size towns usually consider it appropriate to belong to a country club. Residents of coastal areas deem it wise to belong to yacht clubs, but do not attach "I'd rather be sailing" bumper stickers to their cars.

Much thought should be given to selecting a club to join or to try to join. Social standing attached to clubs varies widely, so your decision on what club to join may have a far-reaching effect on your career.

Members of exclusive city dining clubs and country clubs can teach you a great deal about role playing. Practically all of them are masters of the craft. They ooze style and class.

More and more prestigious clubs are finally recognizing the arrival of the twentieth century and allowing women to apply for membership. Pressure should continue to be applied to the holdouts, for being able to invite someone you want to impress for lunch or dinner at the hotsy-totsy club can be extremely valuable in career advancement. So it is worth fighting for. Married women may use the facilities of their husbands' clubs, but lose the clout and prestige individual membership provides. Any woman truly serious about advancing her business career should have her own club membership.

In every city with two or more country clubs, one is known as "The Country Club" to signify its preeminence in the local social pecking order. Any member of "The Country Club" joining a new company must be prepared to suffer short-term pains in order to enjoy long-term gains. Eventually everyone, including the janitor, will learn the connection was made with the help of CEO. Always, CEOs belong to "The Country Club." Quite likely a newcomer to the company who belongs to "The Country Club" will become the target of leading lights who aren't members of that status place. One in such a situation shouldn't worry about the results of the attacks. High Society protects its own. Blue blood is thicker than red.

"The Country Club" is a most exclusive place. There social standing counts for much more than the size of the fortune. How the money was made matters more than how much has been accumulated. Many apply for membership in "The Country Club" but very few make it. Parvenus are especially frowned upon.

Avoid being handed a rejection early in your career. Apply for membership in a club with lesser social status and less picky requirements. When you become recognized as a pillar of the community you can try for "The."

COMMUNITY ACTIVITIES

Being active in community activities and civic organizations provides a plus. Don't become involved in too many lest you be tagged a joiner.

Make sure your spouse is also visibly involved in worthwhile organizations, i.e., those whose active members are featured in the society pages of the local paper. Keep in mind that the more ink you get, the more likely you are to come to the attention of the powers that be.

Both you and your spouse should review periodically all organizations to which you belong. Causes once considered quite acceptable can now be out of favor. What was appealing to a past boss may be appalling to a present one. Make sure all your outside activities fit your current job.

POLITICS

Displaying an awareness of and interest in political developments, known officially as "being politically involved," is vital for anyone seeking to rise to the executive suite. Some CEOs are engrossed in politics. Others have a mild interest and a few, very few, are apolitical. Follow the pace set by your CEO. When expressing political views, make sure you use the same songbook CEO does.

In most companies political involvement consists of participating in intellectual discussions and giving financial support to worthy candidates. Active participation in politics on the local level, such as serving as a precinct captain or as a member of your community's governing body, is usually not helpful in advancing your career and may, in some cases, be a negative. A successful executive must always be an adroit politician without appearing to be one.

If your company has a Political Action Committee, or PAC, become a member at your first opportunity. Be an active and enthusiastic member to further demonstrate your recognition of the need to acquaint candidates for office with the "business point of view." Set a goal of becoming an officer in your PAC as a means of attracting favorable attention from your CEO and other top executives.

YOUR PERSONAL LIFE-STYLE

Bear in mind that "to be successful, you must first appear to be successful." But don't overdo it. There is a big difference between appearing successful and being perceived as excessive. Adopting an ostentatious life-style—eating gourmet foods, jogging, belonging to at least one health club, walking an exotic breed of dog with a cordless telephone in hand, driving a fancy European car, and possessing a taste for expensive wines—can cost you more than money. Such self-indulgence approaching hedonism may endear you to your contemporaries, but it is likely to attract the wrong kind of attention from top executives. At all times act as if you are more interested in your company and your career than you are in self-gratification.

Forget the brownstones, old barns, and warehouses. Live in a nice apartment or condo in the city or in a ranch or Cape Cod house in the suburbs. And make damn sure your lawn and landscaping are attractive. Drive an American-made automobile to demonstrate your unfailing faith in the system.

Keep in good physical condition, but don't follow the hordes to the health clubs. Play racquetball or squash, which are now very "in" games.

Send your kids to private schools (providing the president of the local school board is not a top executive of your company). Entertain your guests stylishly but not exotically or extravagantly. Have a maid come in at least once a week and leave the yard work to a gardener.

CHAPTER 3

CHOOSE THE RIGHT COMPANY

Most companies recognize and reward accomplished role players. Usually you will have as good or better chance of finding fame and fortune in your present company as you would have in another one.

Whether to stay or move to another company is a decision you must make. Here are some specific guidelines to follow in answering this key question.

GUIDELINE 1

Learn the track traveled. Knowing the direction the company is headed and the pace at which it moves is quite important in deciding whether or not it fits you. Some companies move on a fast track, others on a slow track, and still others are trackless—going off in all directions. Fast trackers don't thrive at slow-track companies, and vice versa. Trackless companies are actually ho-hums, masquerading as go-getters. Accomplished role players are especially effective at trackless companies, ones whose operating philosophy changes almost daily.

GUIDELINE 2

Determine who actually runs the Company now, and who is most likely to run it in the future. When applying this guideline keep in mind that success in a number of firms is a relative matter. Sons are most relative and, therefore, most successful. And now daughters are being groomed for top spots.

When you see CEO's nine-year-old child at the office, be extremely kind to the youngster. Today's toddler quickly becomes tomorrow's tycoon.

When CEO has no sons on the scene or daughters interested in inheriting top billing, sons-in-law face equally brilliant futures, providing they don't get caught playing around and thereby incurring the family's wrath. Some nephews make it big. Now and then even a cousin comes to the fore.

If there is a substantial age difference between Father CEO and Crown Prince or Crown Princess, aging leader will likely anoint a surrogate to run the company (at least in name) during the interregnum. Ancient CEO, realizing offspring will be too young to be respected as a leader when the Grim Reaper strikes, elects himself chairman and appoints an amiable and able underling president. Old leader retains most of the power and the stock, doling out a little of each to the surrogate. When Old Ironsides goes to glory, surrogate realizes his dream of taking command. Son or daughter of fallen leader begins to rise rapidly.

Quite a disparity exists in the competence of the people involved in such ploys. Some may be quite able, some only so-so, and others pitifully incompetent. But ability is not at issue here. No competence requirements are attached to eligibility to inherit stock. In family companies, the amount of stock owned, rather than smarts possessed, determines the amount of power wielded. It is essential for role players to understand and accept the fact that a substantial amount of business ineptness is procreated.

Surrogates must be quintessential role players. Day in and day out they must carry out the charade that they really are in charge without evidencing in the slightest how frustrated they really are. Not only are sons or daughters of fallen leaders nipping at their heels, but the Queen Mothers may also be prompting from off stage.

But surrogate leaders certainly "do not go gentle into that good night." Realizing that their power is much more limited than appears on the surface and their time in the spotlight short, they play their role to the hilt.

Anyone presently associated with, or considering catching on with, a company controlled by a family should understand that many other firms offer a lot more potential and a lot less aggravation. Surrogate is the best spot available, but for reasons already detailed, that position can be very vexing. If a surrogate is already on board, one might end up in third or fourth spot providing the switch of allegiance from surrogate to son who will become CEO is made at the right time. Switch too soon and surrogate will lower the boom; do it too late and son won't take a shine to you. A role player is well advised to avoid shows at which the line of succession is already established from here to eternity.

GUIDELINE 3

Learn the management style of the Company. Focus on CEO. He sets the pace.

Ideal CEOs are those who know that they know their business and don't feel compelled to prove anything. They tell you what they expect you to accomplish and let you determine the best way to accomplish it. They judge you on results produced rather than methods employed. But recognize that ideals exist only in fairy tales. Try to pick a company with a CEO who provides underlings with a reasonable amount of autonomy and an opportunity to demonstrate role-playing skills.

Hard-driving, tyrannical, headline-hunting megalomaniacs make good copy for the business press but lousy leaders. For an organizational chart of a firm headed by a despot to be accurate, it would show CEO in a very large box at the top and "Everybody Else" in a box below, far below. All who work for them, even Numbers Two and Three, lead miserable lives. Terming their technique "hands-on management," tyrants call all the shots. All underlings must approach every task on the basis of trying to anticipate the way tyrants want it done rather than the best way to do it. Manufacturers of all antacid medications should send despotic leaders "thank-you" cards at frequent intervals for creating a vast market for their products.

Other top executives almost always mirror the management style of Imperial One. Tyrants insist that their managers also act like sons of bitches at all times. Your immediate boss will make life miserable for you. You, in turn, will be expected to make life miserable for your underlings.

Never give serious thought to joining a show headed by a martinet. If you have made the mistake of joining a one-person company, correct it. Leave now—right now!

CEOs who are sugary sweet one minute, mean as hell the next, are as bad as, possibly even worse than, tyrants. At least you don't have to try to anticipate tyrants' moods. They are always ferocious bastards.

Nice, calm, easy-going CEOs who don't know what is happening are pleasant to be around but create many exasperating and frustrating situations for all underlings. If they know that they don't know, they can be tolerated. If they don't know that they don't know, they should be avoided as much as a tyrant. Both eventually bring disaster.

GUIDELINE 4

Determine if the company operates on the closed- or open-shop principle. Family companies epitomize the closed shop. But closed shops also come in a number of other varieties.

You can't do anything about whether your family owns a company or holds a controlling number of shares for you to inherit. But you may presently possess or be able to acquire qualities requisite for entering a closed shop. Checking carefully as to whether or not your credentials make advancement opportunities available is essential in appraising properly the possibilities of your rising to the top. Here are some examples of closed-shop companies:

Grads of fancy schools only. There are no exceptions to this rule. Comments such as "Some of our best technicians are grads of state universities" translate into "Graduates of state universities are forever technicians in this company."

No grads of fancy schools need apply. This prohibition is as inflexible as is the need for a diploma from a fancy school to become a leading light in some firms. Stemming from more than provincial prejudice, this rule manifests basic insecurities of top executives. Great prescience is not required to determine if grads of hotshot schools are verboten. If no such grads are on board, know that the rule is in effect.

A place for engineers, not poets. Imaginative, creative types thrive in some work environments but wither and shrivel in technical or scientific fields. Do not be deceived by explanations such as "We are seeking to develop a more diverse capability mix. We need more flexibility in our thinking." Effecting such a change may truly be the aim, but such a happening will never come to pass. Engineers, technocrats, and scientists cling firmly and forever to the tenet: "This is the way the books we studied said it should be done, and by God this is the way it is going to be done."

Praise the Lord and pass the bonus check. What the companies operated by conservative born-agains lack in numbers they more than make up for with zealotry. It is because CEOs heading such companies are so fervent in their beliefs and so vociferous in expressing them that it only seems there are more of them than there actually are.

Here the line between God and mammon becomes quite indistinct. Much more emphasis seems to be given to getting rewards to be enjoyed and flaunted in the here and now—earning big incomes and driving fancy cars—than to those only promised in the hereafter. Probably born-again companies operate the most closed shop known to man. If you aren't born again, don't join the choir. "Righteousness and power forge terrible swift swords."

A school-of-hard-knocks kind of place. A vanishing group, but a few, very few, still exist. Most of those who made it to the top without a college degree or even a high school diploma organized their own businesses. A very, very few became CEO in a medium or large business. Usually entrepreneur types brag unabashedly about achieving on their own and gleefully tick off the number of college graduates fired because "they couldn't cut the mustard." (How one cuts mustard remains a mystery.) The business executive sans degree says as little as possible about the educational and social gaps in his or her past. Those with a degree should avoid the former types and those without a degree, the latter.

The composition of the board of directors. Analyze the board of directors' roster thoughtfully and thoroughly. Such an analysis will provide you valuable insight into how the company actually operates. If the board members are proven business leaders from various industries and backgrounds, it is likely a place where genuine goers thrive. If the board includes a black and/or a woman, recognize that management is at least trying to keep up to date. If, however, board members consist almost entirely of relatives, insiders beholden to CEO for pay and position, and second- and third-generation "born leaders" who also belong to "The Country Club," you have not only a closed shop but also a company in a deep rut. Those lacking personal ties to the top, even compleat role players, will find it nearly impossible to penetrate such an elite clique.

Fun or puritan show. An aspect that is much more important than the amount of thought customarily given to it. Learn first the attitude toward consumption of alcoholic spirits considered acceptable. Almost always the established standard reflects the drinking habits of Leader—boozer, social drinker, special occasions partaker, teetotaler, or closet imbiber.

Boozers frequently end up in trouble even in boozing shows. Social or special occasion drinkers encounter the least problems. Teetotalers can make it at shows with a standard of social drinking. Neither boozer, social drinker, nor special occasion partaker can perform well in the hypocritical climate created by a closet drinker.

Not long ago, most business men smoked, usually cigarettes. Not so today. "How can anyone be stupid enough to use anything scientifically demonstrated to be harmful to health?" Even fun shows now frown on cigarette smoking. But some young-tiger types have gone to pot. Others of that same stripe have become confused as to which coke is the real thing.

A sense of humor should be checked at the front door of a puritan show. Fun shows allow humor, but always in moderate doses. Leave the clowning to the clerks.

CHAPTER 4

PAY ATTENTION TO THE PERKS

Rating a better-than-average salary is not enough. No role player can turn in scintillating performances without the stimulus attractive perks provide.

Perks offered should be evaluated on more than their dollar value. First, a perk must be visible so it may be flaunted. Retirement plans, profit sharing, life and medical insurance, sick pay, and subsidized meals are parts of "the hidden paycheck" and should not be confused with or accepted as perks. Executive bonuses and stock purchase or options plans also fall into the same category. All of these and similar offerings should be regarded as forms of compensation—except when discussing them with the Internal Revenue Service. No skilled role player derives any personal gratification from bragging about the outstanding medical insurance coverage the company provides.

Avoid any company that frowns on perks. Worst of all in that nefarious category are those with a stated policy of paying all compensation in cash so each individual may secure desired benefits. At first glance such an approach may appear very free enterprisish, redolent with capitalistic principles. Be ye not deceived.

Such a method of allowing one to pick one's own goodies is anti-American, violating one of this country's most valued and frequently practiced traditions—income tax avoidance. Income is taxable. Most perks are tax free. If the IRS disagrees, a poor memory may overcome the technicalities. Creative record keeping may also be employed, but such a technique is not recommended.

Another good reason for avoiding companies offering all pay and no perks is the subliminal message conveyed: "We are interested only in results." Fortunately, only a few such companies exist.

Perks come in two varieties: ones necessary to perform at peak; desirable ones which can be deferred until later.

NECESSARY PERKS

Expense account. The goose that lays an executive's golden eggs. First, then, determine how loose is the goose. Recognize that policies on expense accounts vary widely. Some places ask no questions, others require notarized receipts for all expenditures exceeding fifty cents, with most businesses somewhere in between these two extremes.

Keep in mind, too, that the numbers mechanics who process expense reports probably do not have an expense account. This deprivation spurs them to trap "expense account abusers" (their term). Don't underestimate numbers mechanics or be deceived by their mild manner. They are very adept at ruining an act. The fewer restrictions placed on how you can spend company money and the fewer records and receipts required, the less difficulty you will have with expense account checkers.

Make sure you are provided a cash advance on your expense account to use as pocket money, commonly called an imprest. Change the t to an s, transform the noun into a verb, and you have its real purpose. To achieve maximum effect from your walking around money, place all bills in an envelope. Men should place it in the inside right pocket of their coats, next to the ever-present pocket secretary, and women should put it at the top of the stuff in their purses. When pulling out the envelope in public, always mention that it is your expense money to reinforce the importance of your position in the company.

American Express card. Obtaining a card nowadays is no big deal. Just be sure you are not given a corporate card which bills all charges for every card holder in your company on one invoice. Get an individual card, with the annual fee paid by the firm.

Why insist on an individual card? The corporate card furnishes the numbers mechanics full details on how much you spent and where you spent it. Sometimes such information can be embarrassing or perhaps downright damaging. But an individual charge from an expensive restaurant which has been declared off limits, or one for another type of indiscretion can be taken care of rather easily by even an average role player.

Go for the American Express Gold for the added prestige and credit privileges it provides. Settle for the green if you must, but never accept a bank credit card in lieu of American Express. Even blue-collar workers have bank cards.

Travel. Not in a designated territory, but the opportunity to go to prestigious places. Your travel should not be of the steady grind type, too frequent or for long periods of time. You should have at least some control over when and where you go.

All travel must be by air. Better not to travel than to go by car. Very few companies permit first-class travel. CEO works all the time he is airborne, requiring the extra room first class provides, so he is exempt. There was a time the no-first-class rule could be evaded by claiming coach was sold out when the reservation was made. Now the rule is to take the next flight on which coach is available.

Company jets are outstanding status builders and favorable impression creators. But don't expect to travel very much in your firm's jet. Be grateful if you make it once. The company's jet is CEO's toy. Usually he is playing with it.

Office. At first it need not be large, fancy, lavishly furnished, or plushly carpeted—but an office it must be. So-called space dividers, regardless of how neatly designed, do not an office make and should not be accepted as a satisfactory substitute.

People at desks in open spaces are branded forever as clerical types. From the day you become an executive you must project the image of a comer, not a clerk.

Secretary. More and more companies are replacing secretaries with word processors and steno pools, so expect to encounter some difficulty in obtaining a secretary of your very own. But persist in your efforts.

To learn why having a private secretary is so important in developing role-playing skills to full potential, stroll through the executive suite. You will not see word processors or steno pools there. But you may very well see two secretaries outside CEO's office, perhaps three. You will notice that all of the top executives have at least one. That's because neither word processors nor steno pools answer telephones, maintain an appointment calendar, or tell a caller that the boss is in a business conference instead of at a three-martini lunch.

Sharing a secretary with one other executive (never more than one) should be agreed to only as a last resort. From day one of secretary-sharing, develop a plan for securing a genuine, honest-to-God private secretary. First, flood the shared secretary with busy work. When your boss asks why a project was not completed on time, say the other one in the tandem had the poor girl (male secretaries are very few and far between) so buried with work she didn't have time to complete your assignments. Stay with your plan of attack until the secretary is yours alone.

Once you have your own secretary, resolve to never let her go. Recognize, however, that efforts will be made to eliminate her, especially if your company follows the management-by-observation philosophy. This practice involves CEO or Number Two periodically sauntering through the halls, ostensibly to rub flesh with the common folk, but actually to determine those who are working, at least those who appear to be, and those who don't even care enough to pretend to be busy.

Those seeking to be known as tough cost-cutters sight in on secretaries as targets for elimination and pay particular attention to their work habits. When a wanderer catches a secretary in the act of loafing, all defenses are judged to be without merit.

An anticipatory offensive plan must be developed to help eliminate personal sightings of your secretary's goofing off. Tell your secretary to do her loafing in the powder room. Wanderer can't go there. If he asks the whereabouts of your secretary, tell him she is doing research work for you at the library.

DESIRABLE, BUT NOT INITIALLY REQUIRED PERKS

Membership in a city, yacht, or country club. If joining another company, work hard on having a paid club membership included in the perk package. If your present company furnishes club memberships, try to become one of the select by giving your boss many reasons why you need access to a club to perform your responsibilities properly.

If you play golf (how well doesn't matter) push extra hard for a company membership. As all players know from experience, the slightest reference to the game automatically brings the question: "Where do you play?" Being forced to reply, "The municipal course," damages both your pride and your chance for promotion.

Membership in a club is not, however, the sine qua non in deciding whether to accept an offer from another company or to stay with your present one. But if membership is too long in coming, borrow the money and buy your own membership. Getting to the top requires belonging to a club. Regard the cost as an investment in your future which will eventually pay big dividends.

Company car. Gone, probably forever, are the big, prestigious, fancy cars. A few companies still offer them as sales contest prizes, but even sales types seem to be turning away from gas guzzlers.

So-called mid-size cars are still socially acceptable, reasonably comfortable, and ridiculously high priced. Catch a mid-size if you can, but settle for a compact if you must.

Before accepting a sub-compact, perhaps more accurately described as a sardine can on wheels, consider two facts very thoughtfully: they are quite uncomfortable, and they offer no status unless they are made outside the U.S.A. and bear an exotic name.

"This is my company car" is a phrase packed with prestige. If your company doesn't furnish cars to anyone, begin promoting the idea. If only a select few are provided this prized perk, use your own car for conducting in-town business. Run up a lot of miles. Soon the numbers mechanics will tire of your being paid so much mileage and suggest to the powers that be that you be included among the chosen few given company cars. If this ploy doesn't work, use your mileage money to buy another car.

Company apartment in an exotic city. San Francisco is the best spot for a pad. Very few companies conduct enough business in "the city by the bay," however, to rationalize, let alone justify, maintaining an apartment there. Most company apartments are in New York City, with Chicago second and Los Angeles third.

A number of business considerations are taken into account in deciding whether or not to rent an apartment in a particular city. All factors are weighed carefully. The final decision is made by CEO on the basis of whether or not he and his wife enjoy visiting that town.

Having access to an apartment in another city builds status for you both inside and outside your firm. Referring to a recent stay in the company's apartment will surely impress your friends. Your associates are certain to regard you as a comer when they learn you have been entrusted with the coveted key.

Company yacht. Quite popular in coastal areas. If your company owns a yacht, access to it is practically required. You will probably not be able to invite other people to ride it, at least not until you become a top executive. But you and your spouse must be invited at least once for you to have any real clout.

Company limousine. Not the kind used only by CEO, but one available to all executives for legitimate, at least semi-legitimate, business purposes.

It need not be a Cadillac or a Lincoln. It doesn't even need to be black, but the driver's uniform should be, so that your friends who see you in the limo realize you are being chauffeured and be properly impressed with your importance.

Use the limo whenever possible for trips to and from the airport. Being picked up at home by the limo will duly impress your neighbors. Arrange for the limo to pick up business contacts at the airport and/or hotel. That you have a say in who is granted such a status symbol is certain to impress them.

Look for opportunities to add to your status through effective use of the limo's phone. Suppose you are a lay leader in your church—as an aspiring role player should be. Call your minister on the limo's phone, informing him you are on your way to Palm Springs (only in winter, of course), where you will speak to a large group of business leaders. Tell him you are calling because you were so impressed by one of his recent sermons that you are going to quote a number of his comments in your remarks, with credit to the source, of course. Soon you will be top lay person in your church.

Executive chair. Very close to being a required perk. Insist on a real executive chair, i.e., one with no space, not even a fraction of an inch, between the bottom of the back support and the seat.

Chairs used by secretaries and clerks have a large gap between back rest and seat. Junior executive chairs have a smaller gap. Pseudo-executive chairs have a gap so slight as to be barely discernible, but should never be accepted as a substitute for a legitimate executive chair with no gap.

Most desirable fabric is leather, genuine of course. The larger the arm rests, the greater the amount of status attached. Vinyl screams "cheap fake." If you are unable to secure real leather, and it is very expensive, settle for a fabric cover in a sedate, executive color.

Telling the "old aching back tale" may produce a chair with no gap. But don't pump that line too hard. Cripples aren't considered comers, nor are chronic complainers.

Pocket calculator. One designed for your particular specialty is best, but always make sure it includes several technological tricks. Buy the one you want and charge it to the company. Plead job necessity if questioned.

Palm Fitting Dictating machine. One of the most impressive accoutrements yet devised, truly a role player's dream. Dictate into the gadget in your car; in fact, anywhere that doing so will make a favorable impression. Even your secretary will be awed when you hand her a tape with the comment: "An idea popped into my head at two A.M., so I got up and taped it before it got away."

Desktop computer. Gives you immediate access to information rather than having to mess with printouts. Such a gadget shouts "I am important." You need not be skilled in computers to use it. The impression it makes is more important than the function served.

Membership in a trade association. Obtaining one should be relatively simple. Most types of businesses not only have a trade group, but also one for most specialties within the industry. In addition, there are organizations such as the Chamber of Commerce and the National Association of Manufacturers which represent all kinds of businesses.

Probably CEO and Number Two do all or most of the

participating in the industry trade association. Your best bet is joining the group offering membership to people engaged in your particular specialty.

National groups are best because they hold meetings in swanky resorts or fancy, big-city hotels. The long cocktail parties and gourmet dinners hosted by suppliers are quite fancy. Ubiquitous hospitality suites offer the assurance no one in attendance will suffer from a dry throat. To eliminate the possibility of suffering nervous breakdowns from overwork, tennis, golf, and tours of the area are provided. Every now and then one of the speakers will even have something important to say.

Well-managed trade associations ensure that business doesn't interfere with the fun. Anyone who must submit a written report on each meeting attended, or is faced with the possibility of having to answer questions about the meeting can partake in the festivities free of fear of being caught. Just buy cassette tapes of the business sessions and listen to them at your convenience.

Some trade associations have both national and regional groups. If you may join both, do it. If you are limited to one, take the national.

Local associations are better than none at all, but just barely. Locals offer only a cocktail hour and dinner at a run-of-the-mill restaurant, usually capped off by a talk by a boring speaker. Worst of all, local meetings are held after business hours, on your own time.

State associations are a slight cut above local ones. Customarily, and all associations are long on custom, each annual meeting is held in the hometown of the current president. Amazingly, most state association presidents hail from Hicksville. So why bother?

CHAPTER 5

PICK A GLAMOROUS INDUSTRY

The type of industry of which your company is a part is also an important consideration. The more glamorous and exciting it is, the better your chances for making it big.

But understand that glamorous and exciting are variables, not constants. Both the airline and automotive industries illustrate how high fliers can sink fast and hot rods run out of gas. When an industry faces problems, some companies do better than others: a General Motors catches cold, a Ford is stricken with pneumonia, and a Chrysler is ill so long that the high cost of treatment requires a form of Medicaid provided indigent companies. An American loses a little altitude, a TWA encounters severe turbulence, and a Braniff crashes.

Glamorous and exciting should not be confused with flashy and ephemeral. Oil exploration flashes at times and flickers at others, depending upon whether OPEC has the spigot turned on or off.

Consider these facts when selecting an industry offering the greatest opportunity to enjoy lots of pay, perks, and prestige.

High-tech industries. Now the most glamorous areas, but a problem is created by the wide difference of opinion as to what constitutes high tech.

Defense industries. Restored to both profitability and respectability by the Reagan administration.

Pharmaceutical companies. The pills may be bitter but the profits are sweet. Even relatively small companies seem to do quite well, regardless of economic conditions.

Advertising. Not nearly as glamorous as it was in the past. Both the so-called "hot shops" and the hotshots who ran them appear to have cooled off considerably. Nevertheless, only superb role players should attempt to perform in advertising.

Wall Street. Still glamorous, but steel nerves and iron stomachs are required. "The Street" is such a closed shop that only consummate role players, preppies preferred, need apply.

Real estate. Despite the sharp ups and downs indigenous to the business, it remains a glamour industry. Although there are usually more losers than winners in real estate deals, with the ratio of losers to winners widening substantially in down markets, the industry remains a magnet to skilled role players. But real estate is a field in which only the quick witted, fast dealing, and thick skinned survive.

Financial institutions. For years untold numbers of people deposited money in banks or savings and loans or bought insurance policies from agents they liked with no questions asked. So steadily did the money roll in that it was practically impossible, even for total incompetents, to screw up established banks, savings and loans, and insurance companies.

Volatile interest rates changed these former havens into competitive jungles. Suddenly, hordes of savers, including many of the unsophisticated variety, withdrew billions of bucks from passbook accounts to put their dollars into higher yielding investments. Many discovered that borrowing on their life insurance was not really a mortal sin punishable by the fires of hell, but actually a wise way to obtain money at a much lower rate than anywhere else. An equally large number of people cashed in old policies and bought new ones which offered a more reasonable return on cash accumulation.

Top flight financial institutions still offer good opportunities. If you choose this field, make sure you pick one that is solid and well managed.

Food. This can be a glamorous industry. But just as the products come in all shapes and sizes, so, too, do the companies engaged in the business. Select one marketing a large number of products on a national scale.

Utilities. Usually quite ho-hum, utilities are too heavily regulated by politicians eager to call attention to themselves through censoring rate increase requests. But the pay is good and plenty of perks sneak by the censors.

Steel. No longer glamorous, but before the flood of imports washed out the domestic industry, steel executives, even junior ones, lived the plush life. Relatively few outsiders were ever impressed by steel, but insiders knew how truly sybaritic life in Steel City was and were content to keep the good life to themselves. Now steel people are singing a new song—"Bring back Smoot–Hawley."

Media. The most glamorous of all industries, truly paradise for role players. Little does it matter that the pay for most is truly picayune, the hours horrendous, and the pressure intense. Each communications medium is an oasis in which the fountain of hope is perpetually full to overflowing. Even those without any realistic chance of having their voices heard on a radio, their faces seen in the movies or on TV, or their names appear above a newspaper or magazine article, cling tenaciously to their fantasy of achieving preeminence someday. Most work very hard, cheaply, and willingly. Many of these forgotten souls are quite accomplished role players. They are merely victims of supply far exceeding demand.

Transportation. Airlines are the most glamorous area, so glamorous, in fact, that many applicants for each opening are always waiting in the wings. To be able to jet around the world for free or at very little cost is naturally appealing to role players. But deregulation and attendant fierce competition which produced fare wars caused many airlines to hit such bumpy air that they cut both pay and perks. So airlines are no longer the high fliers they once were.

Railroads have become part of yesterday. Trucking is too tough for role players.

Chemicals. Too often in the headlines for the wrong reasons—leaks and spills—and the subject of actions by government agencies. No glamour here. Leave chemicals to the scientists!

Manufacturing firms. There may be some roles in marketing which afford good opportunities. But role players will surely bomb out if engaged in the manufacturing process.

Agribusinesses. Completely devoid of the slightest tinge of glamour. Even CEOs in this field, although highly paid and well perked, forever bear the brand of farmer.

Government offices. Totally lacking in glamour and unrewarding in pay and perks, at least those provided over the table. Even most roles in the federal bureaucracy are decidedly humdrum. The few which offer reasonable rewards have many more applicants than vacancies. Top executives in non-glamorous industries can, however, increase substantially their public exposure through accepting appointment to a reasonably high government position, such as an ambassadorship, even if to a small country. The major qualification for this role is a long record of big—really big—contributions to the political party of the man making the appointment.

Management consulting. On the surface, not as glamorous as the media. But those players who can perform in this rather exclusive area are virtually assured of doing quite well. The most glamorous management consulting firms are those with offices throughout the country. Pay is more than good—some call it outlandish. Perks provided are the best available. Genuine management consultants fly first class. The type of work involved is truly a role player's dream—telling others how to run their businesses without being held accountable for the results produced by the recommendations.

Not surprisingly, many CEOs began their business careers with management consulting firms. To earn even a minor part in management consulting requires above average role-playing skills. Only MBAs need apply, with the crimson of Harvard given first consideration. MBAs from night schools with concrete campuses are well advised not to waste their time trying to become associated with a large management consulting firm.

Smaller, regional management consultants are at best considered semi-glamorous. But their standards are less persnickety than those of the well knowns. Average role players have some chance of catching on with smaller, regional firms, providing they demonstrate convincingly the capacity and desire to become exceptional role players.

Computers. Unquestionably the most glamorous of all present industries. Trouble is that computers are presently a case of many being called but few being chosen.

Lots of caution is called for before trying to select a computer company. Many don't survive. The biggies insist that all associates viewed by the public fit their mold. Non-role-player genius types who develop the machines are kept in cages and fed raw meat twice a day. Anyone with the slightest inclination to demonstrate individualistic tendencies occasionally is well advised to try another type of business.

Electronics. An industry so huge that the degree of glamour attached varies sharply according to the product marketed—from zero to very high. The mysterious chip produced in California's Silicon Valley, where new millionaires allegedly emerge every day, is very glamorous. Positions in electronics available to role players are in marketing, not product development.

Retailing. Can be very rewarding and even glamorous. But even consummate role playing may not be enough to get to the top here. Competition is so intense that leading players' performances are actually judged on results produced. All is not lost for role players attempting to become executives in retailing. At least they can acquire the proper wardrobes at a discount.

Natural resources. A mixed bag. Oil is very glamorous to investors when the supply is low, profits high, and the stock price out of sight, but it is continually maligned by the consumers who pay the high prices. Both pay and perks provided actors in the oil business more than offset any barbs received or embarrassment experienced. Even though coal has made a dramatic comeback, it is still considered a dirty business. It is difficult, if not impossible, to find any glamour in a two-by-four or a piece of paper, so timber remains strictly run-of-the-mill.

Hotels and restaurants. Usually offer more drudgery than glamour. Top spots are very scarce. Getting to the top requires performing menial tasks for a long time and working many, hard hours. One must show great patience, both in working with the underlings, whose average length of service is about three weeks, and enduring irate customers, many of whom are plain drunks. Being general manager of a large, fancy resort hotel is a suitable reward for accomplished role players. But the chances of getting such a position are minimal.

Alcoholic beverages. Sort of a so-so—not so bad in enlightened areas and not so good in the Bible Belt. Role players must engage in marketing, never in manufacturing. Not only must one be a skilled role player to sell booze, but one must also be very tough. Sometimes there's a bit of pushing and shoving involved in getting a brand on the shelves. Pick a big company, since small ones seem to be losing their kick.

CHAPTER 6

PREPARE YOURSELF TO SUCCEED

Before seeking a promotion in your present company or a position with another firm, answer two key questions:

1. Do I have my act together? (If answer is yes, move on to question two. If you don't have your act together, reread chapter 2 and get it together fast.)
2. Do my present company and industry offer me the opportunity to move to the top? (If answer is yes, use the methods outlined in this chapter for being picked for promotion. If not, reread chapters 3, 4, and 5 to be certain you next try a company and industry in which your role-playing abilities can reach full bloom.)

In seeking to be promoted or in presenting your talents to another company, you must concentrate on these two most important aspects of role playing:

1. *speaking style*
2. *self-confidence and poise—best described as savoir faire.*

If, in time, you do not excel in these areas, you will have no chance, absolutely none, of reaching the executive suite. In fact, you may encounter difficulty in holding on to what you have.

That these two qualities are important shouldn't come as a shock. Think about the stars of stage, movies, and television. What separates these national heroes from the muddling masses? Their speaking style and poise, of course.

Consistently perfect are the tone, diction, word rate, and vocal variety of the stars. They attract and retain attention with their speaking styles. Would-be leaders in business must learn to do likewise. Immediately eliminate ah-ah or er-er, the long pause, the half-completed sentence, and stammerings and stutterings.

Watch the stars' mannerisms while they perform. They maintain constant eye contact with the audience or camera. They never shift their weight from one leg to the other, rock back and forth on their heels, fiddle with their fingers, twiddle with a ring or watch, stroke their chins, or play with their nose or ears. They are so calm, so very sincere, that one automatically accepts their every word as gospel.

Read and reread this chapter. Practice each aspect until you are convinced you are performing at peak level. Once you know what to do, and how to do it well, you are on your way to becoming a rising star.

METHOD OF SPEAKING

Focus on the how. Send to all your brain cells the message: "*How* I speak is much more important than *what* I speak." Keep repeating the message until the how reflexively receives top priority. Soon you will notice that your listeners are concentrating more on your method of speaking than the thoughts you are expressing. You are beginning to create the desired effect, what role playing is all about. Don't stop. Rehearse, rehearse, rehearse. You are only on the first step of the stairway to the top. You still face a long trek.

Observe the experts. Professional motivational speakers epitomize the great benefits to be derived from concentrating on the how and letting the what take care of itself. If you live in a fairly large city, very likely a so-called "motivational caravan" makes a one-night stand at least once a year. Be sure to attend the next one held in your town. If you live within driving distance of one, make the trip.

Don't be concerned about having to wait as long as a year for a caravan to come to your area. Role playing requires patience as well as commitment. Nor should you allow the seemingly high price of a ticket to raise second thoughts about attending. Consider the cost an investment in career enrichment. Apply the same reasoning to traveling to attend a caravan, even if an overnight stay is involved.

During the sessions, glue your eyes on each speaker. Carefully observe mannerisms, facial expressions, and gestures. Attune your ears to the word rate, inflections, switch in pitch, dramatic pauses, and so forth. Give your thought processes a leave of absence. Ignore the content of the messages.

You won't be allowed to tape these sessions, but you can either buy tapes of all the talks after the show is over or order them to be sent to you. At the very least, buy or order tapes of those speakers you consider top performers.

When playing the tapes, be concerned only with content. Carefully evaluate the soundness of ideas expressed, the depth of the thinking underlying the words, and the validity of the philosophy advocated. Do not be a role player in this act. Analyze each speaker's ideas as honestly and objectively as you can.

Now compare the results of your objective analysis of each speaker to that of your initial reaction. This exercise should convince you how much the how and how little the what count in making a favorable impression.

Women should use much caution in selecting experts in speaking style and confident manner to emulate. The emergence of women in significant roles in business has spawned a large group of instant experts telling women what to say and how to say it. A few are excellent, some good, and others far from good. Better to ignore novices and copy women who have proven themselves as top performers.

Check your word rate. Probably word rate is the single most important factor in speaking style—the more rapid the rate, the more favorable the impression created. There are, of course, exceptions to this rule. But in general, rapid-fire, unhesitating speakers constitute the vast majority of outstanding role players.

Members of fundamentalist churches have a decided advantage in developing a rapid word rate. Brothers and sisters from Texas and Oklahoma appear to have acquired an extra edge. Those from other border states seem to have the rapid-fire delivery mastered, too. Most of the Deep South folks have too much of a drawl, but a few outstanding rapid-word-raters can be found in the heart of Dixie.

Sunday after Sunday, fundamentalists have listened to their ministers preach on salvation and damnation at a rate approaching the speed of sound. Their only pauses are those designed to convey convincingly the joys of heaven and the pains of hell. Without realizing it, many members of fundamentalist congregations have acquired the speech patterns of their preachers. From faithful attendance at Sunday services they learned an important lesson beyond those contained in the Scriptures—the quantity of words far outweighs the quality of ideas.

Not all fundamentalists are rapid-word-raters, nor are all rapid-word-raters fundamentalists. It isn't really important how you learn to talk rapidly. What counts is that either you now talk that way or you learn to talk rapidly, yet distinctly, as soon as possible.

Check your progress. Test yourself before an interview, meeting, or other important engagement. Plot out mentally how to sell yourself to your boss or the personnel director of another company. Practice until you are satisfied with your presentation. Then tape it and listen to it very critically.

Count the pauses and stammers. Listen carefully for insipid expressions such as "you know," "I mean," "OK?" and "see what I mean." Check to determine if you switched pitch frequently and emphasized your most important thoughts. Make sure you spoke rapidly but distinctly.

Repeat the taping and critical analysis until you are completely satisfied that your performance will make a good impression. You'll be amazed how much and how quickly this exercise has improved your speaking style. If by the twentieth time you are still not performing satisfactorily, you may want to consider engineering or some scientific field.

Timing yourself with a stop watch will help you quicken your word rate. But listen carefully to the tape to make sure you sound natural and at ease. Talking rapidly must appear natural to be truly effective. Never exceed your speed limit.

Deal with an accent. Southern drawls, Southwestern twangs, or Eastern accents pose no problems for those performing in their home regions. It is a definite advantage to be recognized as "one of us" rather than someone who "talks funny."

Southern drawls have an almost universal charm, but aren't highly regarded by the Eastern establishment. Anyone from the South who moves to the East should retain a little, but lose most, of the drawl that comes with the territory. A little is charming, a lot considered "cracker." Southwestern twangs are transferable only to the Deep South. "Idear" or "cah" goes over only in the East.

If you are transferred to an area in which an accent prevails, don't acquire it. Your associates will judge you as an obvious poseur. If you move from an accent area to a non-accent location and you are concerned that your "funny talk" is detracting from your acceptance, consider enrolling in one of the "accent removal courses" now being offered in increasing numbers.

Speech delivered with an accent foreign to American shores brings friendly smiles in public but produces disgusted frowns in private. Although eliminating a foreign accent is quite difficult, the effort should be made to try to minimize it. Some may say Henry Kissinger did all right with his German accent, but he made his mark in academe and government. Keep in mind that his brother, Walter, who made it big in business, speaks practically accent free.

Deepen the tones. A deep voice is preferred, medium-deep tolerated, and high pitched equated with Mickey or Minnie. Anyone suffering from the high-pitched malady should immediately seek a cure. Visit a speech therapist. Consult a nose-and-throat specialist. If these and all other sources of possible remedies do not lower the pitch and deepen the tones, consider applying to some type of medical school. All doctors, regardless of voice qualities, are accorded status and prestige.

CONFIDENCE AND POISE

Your self-confidence and poise will increase automatically as your speaking style becomes more effective. The two work in tandem. The more confident you appear, the more authoritative you sound, the better the impression you make.

Learn from the masters. For proof of the benefits derived from self-confidence, one need look no further than those true paragons of poise, the Wall Street types—investment bankers, financial analysts, and stockbrokers. Accomplished masters are they of conveying the conviction: "I say, therefore it is." One certainty can be counted on when they talk: qualifiers and disclaimers such as "I think," "Perhaps," "I am not certain," and "I blew that one" will never cross their lips. Rather, you will hear only "I know," "It will," "I'm sure," and "That happened because."

How are they able to speak consistently with infallibility on all matters involving the most uncertain and unpredictable of businesses? How do they explain previous predictions which turned out to be entirely wrong in a way that convinces they were right all along? Through their unequaled savoir faire, that's how. That their act works so well proves conclusively the almost unlimited power of self-confidence and poise.

Learn now, and impress the lesson indelibly in your mind: the humble never make it to the top. The Bible tells us that the meek shall inherit the earth. When that passage is quoted to prove the merits of humility, seasoned role players respond: "They damn well better, for that is the only way they will ever get it."

You are judged according to what you are perceived to know. Act as if you know a lot, but not as if you are a know-it-all.

Don't confuse cockiness with confidence. In seeking to make good impressions, never mistake loud and/or incessant talk for an effective speaking style, or blatant arrogance for savoir faire. Use I, me, or mine in moderation. The executives you are trying to impress have massive egos. Don't step on them.

As you move up the ladder, it is permissible, but not required, to raise your voice a few decibels (but never to a scream) and to express your ideas and opinions in a manner conveying that they originated on Mount Sinai. Commanding attention and giving the impression you know what you are talking about are the most effective means of acquiring authority and power—next to inheriting them.

Know your audience. After establishing yourself either at a new company or on a promotion path in your present one, always keep in mind that you give one type of performance to subordinates and quite another kind to superiors. It is perfectly OK to interrupt a subordinate, but really dumb, sometimes disastrous, to start talking when your boss is in mid-sentence.

Your mission with the masses is to instill in them the notion that you are the boss, and all operations are going to be handled your way. Every word to the elite, however, should be based on impressing them with your exceptional ability and your capacity to assume more responsibility.

Your goal is to be tagged as one who knows all that is known about the subject under discussion. Answering questions from on high with "I'm not sure," "I think so," "I'll have to check on that," will mark you as one who doesn't know what is happening.

Education has been defined as "the transformation of cocksure ignorance into thoughtful uncertainty." An elevating thought, this, one ringing with honor and truth in the halls of academe. In executive suites and boardrooms it evokes a hearty laugh. Wise ones know from long experience that in business, confidence equates with correctness.

CHAPTER 7

APPEAR IMPRESSIVE

To have any chance of being promoted or obtaining a better position with another company, you must first *look* like an executive. No matter if your resume is most impressive, your speaking style overpowering, or your savoir faire almost blinding, your clothes and personal appearance must—absolutely must—fit the position you seek to fill.

First impressions trigger final judgments. The initial impression of you formed by the personnel director and others involved in the selection process are necessarily based on your personal appearance. After all, they can't look into your head and measure the size of your brain; they have no machine to measure your ambition and decision-making ability. Later, the company shrink may attempt to gauge your assets in these areas. But for now the analysis is limited to auditing your manner of speaking, assessing your savoir faire, and looking you up and down.

Pay close attention to each item of your attire. If you are being considered for a promotion, thoroughly analyze the attire of those in that or a similar job. When interviewing at another company, case the place in advance or seek the advice of friends familiar with that operation. If you have been selected by a head hunter, ask for advice on what type of outfit would be appropriate. If you must go into the interview with little or no knowledge of the tastes of the hierarchy, take the conservative route. It is quite difficult to err in business by being too conservative.

Pay close attention to all of your clothing, not just part of it. Tacky shoes or a gravy-stained tie or scarf can ruin an expensive suit or dress.

It is always better to concentrate on quality rather than quantity when selecting your wardrobe. It is not only OK, but in fact advisable, to add a distinguishing personal touch or two—as long as you don't attract the wrong kind of attention.

MEN

Shoes. Solid color, matching your suit, is the only type to be considered. Two-tones are taboo. Built-up heels shout "short man complex." Buckles, even tassels, are now acceptable, even in the inner circle.

Wall Street types are fond of wearing cordovans with dark suits. Only these accomplished role players can turn this trick without being labeled hick.

White shoes come and go. Only preppies can wear them without raising eyebrows, but even these outstanding role players can put themselves at risk by wearing white. The same caveat applies to oxfords.

Stick to leather. Wear no alligators, real or fake. Leave all boots, even those which cover only the ankles, to cowboys.

Shoes must be fairly new, shined, and free of cuts or scratches. Avoid the down-at-the-heels look.

Add some status to your shoes. With a black grease pencil put a number, say 323, at the bottom of each sole near the heel. Make the numbers large so they may be seen easily. If you have access to a machine which prints numbers on plastic strips, so much the better.

During your interview, cross your legs so the number is

visible. Those you are trying to impress will recognize immediately that 323 is the number of your locker at your country club. Those who don't know what the number signifies aren't worth impressing. Do not keep your legs crossed too long lest you wrinkle your trousers.

Socks. Your only choice is solid-color, over-the-calf varieties. No pastels or argyles, please. Anyone giving a thought to wearing white should immediately close this book and give it to a friend. Fallen over-the-calf stockings expose more than your leg. Check the elastic at each wearing or buy garters. Make sure the color of your stockings matches your suit.

Jacket and trousers. A suit is always better than a blazer or sport coat and slacks, even in offices not requiring suits. Solid darks are best, with thin stripes a close second. Tweeds and herringbones are OK, but checks and plaids are dangerous. One dark brown suit is acceptable. Tans, greens, and light grays are suitable for wearing at agricultural expositions.

If your office permits sport jackets, use the privilege sparingly. Stick with black or navy blue blazers and camel's hair or tweed jackets. Don't put elbow patches on any of your jackets until you have become an exceptional role player.

Don't put glasses, pens, or pencils in the breast pocket of your jacket. Make sure your side pockets do not bulge. In areas subjected to winter's chill, wear only wool. In summer, cool off with a combination of wool and synthetic, never pure synthetic. The so-called double knits can snag your career.

Overcoat. This *must* be full length. Car coats are only for nonbusiness occasions. Trench coats are strictly for TV private eyes. Leave the fur-collar variety to outdoorsmen. A camel's hair coat is a must for a role player performing in climes which require overcoats. As you move up the ladder, make it cashmere. Leave those with shoulder straps to the generals.

Hats. Although many, perhaps most, now go hatless, true executives have one to wear on business trips. No hound's tooth patterns and/or feathers on the side are allowed. Caps are a bit too cute. Leave the fur to the Russians.

Shirts. White remains the safest color. Solid light blues are acceptable. Button-downs are always in for business wear, but are definitely not for social events.

You can add a touch of class to your shirts in several ways. Buy those with deeper-than-average collars or have your shirts custom-made. Both types cost more than regular shirts, with the custom-made varieties involving considerable outlay. If you decide to invest in custom-made shirts, request no pocket. Have your shirtmaker embroider your initials where the pocket would have been. Initials on a cuff are a negative—much too gaudy.

Thin red, blue, or green stripes on white broadcloth or oxford are fine. Wide stripes, checks, or other loud styles are forever banned. White collars on light blue shirts fall into the same category as elbow patches on jackets—only for very skilled role players. White collars on stripes are too much even for skilled role players.

French cuffs are considered the sole province of top executives, so members of the supporting cast should not wear them at the office. As it is still OK for lesser lights to wear French cuffs on social occasions, keep several on hand. Make sure your cuff links are tasteful. Gimmick types, such as naked ladies, may bring a laugh to your face, but comments about them made behind your back can hurt you.

Pay close attention to your shirt collar. A collar pointed upward creates the same impression as does a copy of *Successful Farming* protruding from your pocket. Find a laundry that knows how to starch a collar, or stick to button-downs. Collar pins can help, and they add a bit of class.

Ties. Rep silk ties are always good, except with striped suits or shirts. Bright pastels or flowered patterns have no place except in the trash can. Stick to silk. One knit may be more than enough. Synthetics should be worn only at family reunions. Darker colors help minimize the inevitable gravy stains.

The four-in-hand knot is used most frequently by those who count. It is OK to tie by the Windsor method, providing the knot isn't the size of an orange.

The end of the tie should always be at the top of the belt. Preferably, the tie ends meet, but the bottom must never be longer than the top.

Bow ties convey eccentricity. Professional types, academics, and Southern politicians can get by wearing them. So can the owner of a company. He may or may not be eccentric, but he doesn't give a damn.

Whether or not to buy ties with initials or distinctive designs at the bottom is a most important decision. If you can afford them, buy the very best. Try to own at least one or two, even if you must scrimp a bit, but never buy the cheap imitations. Company ties are now in vogue. Become a walking signboard only if your boss or CEO wears one.

Always wear a tie bar. Floppy ties signal sloppy habits. Diamonds or pearls on the tie bar or pin shout "promoter type." Fakes of either are unthinkable. Avoid emblems, even those of your company, unless you risk being tagged as a non-team player.

Underwear. The one item you can wear what you damn well please.

Jewelry. In general, the less jewelry worn, the better. A wedding ring is expected. Not having one raises suspicions of either unsettled conditions on the home front or possessing a liking for the ladies. College or fraternity rings are quite acceptable. Indian rings, bracelets, or watch bands may be worn in the Southwest whence they came, but nowhere else. Only certain types can wear a pinky ring with the style and grace it is supposed to convey. If you aren't the pinky type, and you will know the minute you put one on, forget it.

Diamonds should be worn only by wheeler dealers. If you are in a business bearing that stigma or distinction, depending upon one's attitude toward wheeling and dealing, wear it. The diamond ring of a real estate operator flashes,

"This guy knows how to put a deal together"; one on a banker cautions, "Watch him, he may have his hand in the vault."

Belt buckles should be plain and simple. Those with designs and emblems should be worn only at drag races and tractor pulls.

Wear an attractive, quality wristwatch, but an obviously very expensive one may raise unnecessary questions.

Never wear a lapel pin, even one with your company's logo.

Hair. Whether or not you are promoted or selected by another company often turns into a hairy situation, so pay very close attention to the hair on your head, face, even your hands.

Should you have a regular haircut or fancy style? As a general rule of thumb, a regular haircut makes fewer waves and is, therefore, seen more frequently in executive suites. Make sure your barber doesn't feature the "bucolic buffoon" look. The "Princeton cut" continues to be popular with leading players. Crew cuts scream "no class." Only clerks and clowns wear them.

Hair styles are OK if not extreme. The trick is to have the neat, orderly appearance which a style gives without looking styled. Avoid heavy hangings over the ears and eyes. Applying globs of hair spray gives the glued-down rather than dry look.

Not even exceptional role players can get by with a permanent. Leave the curls to the TV newscasters.

Don't abandon the wet look too hastily. It is especially suitable for those with high foreheads and thick glasses who simply can't handle the dry look.

Should a bald man wear a toupee? Yes, if he begins wearing it before the bald label is applied, and the wig is of high quality and closely matches the color of the original crop. If you are presently bald or can't afford a top quality wig, learn to live with your baldness.

Even though mustaches have made a strong comeback, don't rush to the hirsute lip. First determine if mustaches are worn by any of the top executives. Let your answer be your guide. Thin mustaches are most accepted, full ones frowned upon, and the handlebar variety strictly for cowboys and college professors. A mustache grayer than the hair on the head immediately creates doubts as to whether the hair color is solely the work of Mother Nature.

Anticipating the ravages of time can keep the actual color of your hair a secret between you and your barber. At the first sign of gray, start dyeing. Then you are in control. You can retain the original color as long as you want. When you are ready for gray, dump the dye.

Gray sideburns seem to enjoy much greater status and respectability than does gray on top. If you have gray sideburns, leave them alone. If you seek a more mature look, add a touch of gray to the sides.

Leave all dye jobs to professionals. Your appearance is too important to be a do-it-yourself project.

Keep sideburns above middle ear. Leave long ones and "lamb chops" to professional wrestlers and bronco busters.

Beards are now more acceptable, albeit grudgingly. Scientific, technical, and artistic types can get by with one, but a beard is still regarded as belonging in barrooms, not board rooms. Forget it!

Handkerchiefs. For your interview, one handkerchief is not enough. Take two—one for the front right pants' pocket. This is not frivolous advice, but may in fact be the most useful pointer in this chapter.

No matter how self-confident and poised you are on the outside, how well rehearsed or satisfied you are with your performance, you are bound to experience inner tenseness while you are jumping through the hoops held by the personnel director. Tenseness always creates sweaty palms. Nothing brings rejection faster than sweaty palms.

Experts in personnel selection equate sweaty palms with practically every character flaw known or imagined—insecurity, dishonesty, instability, cowardice, and indecisiveness. Eliminate all possibility of being suspected of possessing any of these despicable traits. Use the handkerchief in your front pants' pocket to wipe the perspiration from your hand after each handshake. When introduced to two or more people at once, don't wipe after each shake lest you disclose the true source of your strong character. Rather, after each shake, slide your hand down the side of your trousers to ensure that your palms are sweat free. So you get another big benefit from wearing a dark suit to the tryout. The sweat won't stain your trousers.

Don't display a handkerchief in the breast pocket of your jacket. Only a few top leaders now follow that practice. Your having one may be regarded as a bit too hotsy totsy.

Glasses. On first thought it may seem that glasses are glasses are glasses. Think again. The style of glasses worn is considered to be indicative of the character and personality of the individual wearing them. If yours can be construed as extreme to even a slight extent, buy new ones. Select a conservative style in a neutral color. Heavy black frames scream "poseur." To make certain you are selecting the proper frames, check the style worn by top executives.

If you use half-glasses for reading, don't wear them while performing. This style makes everyone look like the Ancient Mariner. You may need to read during your interview, and if you can't read without squinting (which wrinkles your face), buy full-frame reading glasses.

Briefcase. An essential part of your costume. Make sure yours fits your role. Avoid the commonplace. Role players must stand out from the herd. Carry one which is attractive and practical, but not too fancy. Focus attention on your act, not your briefcase.

WOMEN

Contrary to much of the advice given women in business on how to dress for maximum effect, the fact is that a woman should dress like a woman, and not always drape herself in suits, shirt blouses, and cute little stringy ties. Many of the manuals on this subject stress wearing pinstripes, shirt blouses, and "neat" little bow ties. Those who follow such advice risk being caricatured as feminine versions of the look-alikes for which a large computer firm is so well known.

Strike a balance between mannish dress and feminine frills, and in the process retain a heap of femininity.

Dress appealingly, but not too fancily. Cover all parts adequately, but not nun-like, to keep attention focused on your brains and business savvy rather than your feminine attributes.

Shoes. Stick to closed pumps, color-keyed to the outfit you are wearing. Go with heels, even if you are tall—being able to look down on a male boss can be a subtle power tool. Avoid flats and faddish styles. Let the clerks flaunt them. Leave boots to waitresses and cowgirls.

Stockings. Stick to neutral shades. Leave black and pastel shades to chorus girls and whites to nurses.

Suits. Some styles are fine; just make sure your suit doesn't look like an exact copy of your rivals'. Buy suits of good quality which don't appear extravagant. You don't need to stick to dark, conservative colors; have a red and/or green suit in your wardrobe. Don't always wear a "neat" little tie with your suit. Avoid tweeds and other fabrics which may be a bit too masculine. Four-in-hand ties are also too mannish. Pants suits aren't for executives.

Dresses. Perfectly acceptable, in fact some are required. Attractive dresses can provide a big boost in role playing. When two women, one in a suit, blouse, and tie, the other in an appealing silk dress, are making a presentation to the leading players, put your money on the one in the dress making the more favorable impression, assuming both are about equal in speaking style and savoir faire.

Blazers and skirts. Quite effective. Avoid blazers with crests and shields. Sweater-vests are also OK. Pullover sweaters may be too revealing.

Coats. Furs are perfectly acceptable on cold days. Make sure yours is long enough to cover the hem of your skirt or dress, but not so long that it reaches your ankles. Leave that variety to the movie stars. Dark furs are more chic than white or gray. A camel's hair polo coat is always in vogue.

Hair. Wear the style you think best suits you. Avoid frizzy permanents or mannish hair cuts—both attract the wrong kind of attention. Use much caution when dyeing to another color. If you go the blonde route, make sure your roots are covered at all times. Touching up a bit of premature gray is perfectly acceptable, as long as it is not done in stovepipe black. Wigs are strictly passé.

Jewelry. A little goes a long way. Large, garish rings or bracelets indicate too much of a push for recognition. Pearls and fancy necklaces should be left at home for after-hours events. Charm bracelets may be a bit too brassy.

Makeup. Go easy here so as not to earn the sobriquet "painted lady." Leave eye shadow and painted eyelids to the TV models who peddle the stuff. Skip artificial fingernails and extremely long natural ones. Avoid bright nail polish.

Glasses. Take the conservative route. Neat horned rims are best. Putting them on your hair when not in use is cool, even suave. Don't hang them from a chain around your neck—too schoolmarmish. Granny glasses are outdated.

Purse. Ignore the advice about carrying only a billfold. Carry a purse of moderate size. Make sure it isn't overloaded or messy in case you need to open it in the presence of top executives. Appearing untidy or disorganized brings bad reviews.

Briefcase. A must! Just make sure it is attractive and not so large that you look overburdened while carrying it.

Hats. No!

Perfume. Never at the office.

Underclothing. You're on your own here. A man offering advice on this subject would be a damn fool.

CHAPTER 8

GET ATTENTION IN THE INTERVIEW

Throughout his youth, Abraham Lincoln's motto was: "I shall prepare myself; my time shall come." He did. His time did.

Start immediately to prepare yourself to win when your time comes to be scrutinized for promotion or for a better position in another company.

Practice your speaking style by using a tape recorder and evaluating your rate of improvement. Work hard on projecting self-confidence and poise. Make sure your personal appearance always meets specifications.

From the moment you meet the fate decider, be he or she Top Star, personnel director, CEO's aide de camp, or your immediate boss-to-be, put on a good act. Do the standard routines—shake hands firmly (with dry palms), maintain eye contact, stand and sit straight, and exude confidence and poise.

While exchanging the customary inanities, quickly determine the approach most likely to produce desired reactions. First, try to find out who is going to make the decision, then concentrate your efforts on that decision maker. If CEO is present, or you are going to visit with him later, your task is easy. He will! If a committee will make the final judgment, play to the strongest member.

Avoid coming on as an eager beaver. Act as if you are a buyer, not a seller. Subtly convey your conviction that if you don't get this promotion some other firm will make you an offer, or if this company doesn't hire you, your future at your present job is very bright.

From the beginning of the interview, act as if your ability to handle the job is a given. Your aim is to make your fate decider ask: "How can we keep this person?" or "How can we hire this person?"

WINNING A PROMOTION

Develop a source of reliable information on what better positions are going to be available so you can prepare yourself before the openings become common knowledge. Form a close friendship with someone in the Personnel Department who can and will serve as your pipeline. Curry the favor of anyone who might be able to help you move up the ladder.

When a better position than you presently hold opens up, one for which you are reasonably qualified or at least think you are, pass the word to your friends in high places that you are ready and able to fill the spot. Don't directly ask them for help, but leave the impression that if you are not advanced soon you will have to start listening to some of the offers you are receiving from other companies.

In promotion situations, you have the advantage of knowing your fate decider, if not personally, at least by reputation. Concentrate on those aspects of your background and work experience which hit the hot button and avoid those which activate the turn-off switch.

SEEKING A BETTER POSITION

Make contacts with lots of people outside your company to uncover desirable openings. When you succeed in obtaining an interview, turn on all of your charm. Seek out some common ground with the decision maker. Fraternity brotherhood or sorority sisterhood can provide a big boost. Keep probing for a mutual interest or experience.

Even if you literally despise your present job, praise the firm and its leading executives. Stick to this line even if you are being "outplaced." Use such high-sounding phrases as "I neither regret my past nor bemoan my present"; "I have a bright future with ABC. I am here to learn if XYZ offers me a brighter one."

If you are considering moving to a smaller company in the same line of business, you have a ready-made act for impressing CEO of the smaller firm. He drools at the thought of attracting someone from the biggies, for in the business world, being big equates with being good.

When talking to CEO of the smaller company, always refer to executives of the big company by their first names. He probably knows them and may respect them.

Puff your present job. Talk big numbers. Citing figures such as earnings will help convince CEO that if you can handle a somewhat important position with a large company you are ready for a big job in his company. But you can trip yourself while performing this routine. Never use the words "small" or "little" when talking to CEO about his company, for it follows in the logic of business that if big is good, small must be bad. If size comparisons are brought up, and let him do the bringing up, tell him "You are not quite as large as my present company."

Immediately demonstrate that you have thoroughly checked the company's background and growth rate. Obtain some facts and figures to toss around in the interview, even if you have to get them from the receptionist while you are waiting for the cross-examination to begin. Be sure to tell CEO how impressed you are with the very favorable reputation his company enjoys throughout the business community.

Add credence to the fiction you are there to buy the job rather than sell yourself by asking CEO what the company's specific operating philosophy is or what makes it different from others in the same industry. You won't receive a direct answer, but you will impress the hell out of CEO.

YOUR SESSION WITH THE SHRINK

Part of the selection process at most companies, regarded as a sacred ritual, not a mere formality, is the visit with the company shrink, known officially as the consulting psychologist. Always approach this encounter in a serious manner. Avoid all indications of flippancy while with the shrink. Regard the session as a formidable hurdle you must clear in order to be hired.

Advance preparation for your encounter must be rigorous and intense. Recognize that the shrink must reject some applicants to justify the fee which, to put it delicately, is substantial. To get in shape, think very hard about the characteristics usually associated with the position you are seeking. Then practice affecting those desired traits you do not presently possess.

One aspect of the encounter is totally predictable—the shrink's smiling at you, shaking your hand, and going all out to put you at ease. He or she begins by assuring you that the main purpose of the interview and the testing is to help determine if the job offered is right for you, not if you are right for the job.

Shrink carefully measures your reaction to this avuncular approach to determine if you are really buying or in fact selling. Maintain the same facial expression during the interview. A dead pan is a role player's greatest asset; a face revealing actual feelings, the biggest liability. Don't cringe, flinch, or exhibit any trace of uneasiness.

Throughout the session follow what you have learned from this book on speaking effectively and appearing confident. Continually display the characteristics associated with the position you seek: outgoing and enthusiastic for marketing; contemplative and phlegmatic for accounting and finance; quick witted and dynamic for executive responsibilities. Imagine you already have the job, then speak and act accordingly.

Use all the allotted time for completing any written tests. Regardless of how stupid some of the questions seem—and some will seem very stupid—do not give any flippant answers. Respond in the way common sense tells you.

Beware of land mines—shrinks call them "lie factors"—in the questions. Maintain the same characteristics throughout. Don't be an extrovert on page one and a shrinking violet on page two.

Be careful with the drawings, avoiding flourishes and fancies. Keep them simple and sincere. Your drawings mean precisely what the shrink says they mean. The plainer and straighter your drawings, the more likely the shrink will be to judge you a straight.

You will not receive a yea or nay from the decision maker until the shrink provides a report on what is going on inside your head, known officially as a "psychological profile." In all likelihood, the shrink's report is heavily relied upon, not because it contains such valuable information, but rather because it costs so much.

After following this advice, you probably succeeded in getting promoted or winning the new position. If you didn't, go back to Chapter 1 and start over.

CHAPTER 9

PICK THE RIGHT PROPS

When you are promoted, squeeze all the attention you can out of the big moment. CEO should send a memo to all those on your level and above informing them of the importance of your new assignment and your outstanding qualifications for it. If he doesn't do it, take the initiative. Draft the memo for him. Tell him spreading the word on your ascendancy is part of good business communications—a term equated with heaven, home, and mother.

Do all you can to make certain the next edition of the company's magazine includes a fitting write-up and flattering photo of you. Get as many column inches as you can to make your new position appear quite important. Read the article before it is printed. Don't be bashful (a luxury role players can't afford) about suggesting additions which portray you as a classy comer.

Your photo should be of fairly recent vintage and show you in proper attire. If your most recent one doesn't meet these specifications, have a new one taken and charge it to the company. Order a good supply of prints for future publicity releases and two extras—one for your spouse and the other for your mother.

Keep after the publicity people to write and send news releases to local media and your college's alumni magazine. Insist that a photo be sent to all print media. PR people usually attach importance only to activities involving CEO or themselves, but they are usually exceptional role players and respect other good performers. Let them know you are a force to be reckoned with, but don't try to run over them. You'll need them to publicize your future promotions.

YOUR COMING-OUT PARTY

When moving to another company, do all of the above plus one: prepare yourself carefully for your introduction to your peers and the top executives. The type of welcome you receive will indicate pretty accurately both the importance placed on your position and the caliber of your new company.

Classy companies host a cocktail party or reception to present new executives. If local board members are invited, know that your future is indeed bright. Next in prestige is the luncheon in the executive dining room hosted by CEO.

At your debut you will be asked to make a few remarks. Make sure they are few. Your mission is to impress the leading players without annoying your peers. Use your role player's speaking style and display your savoir faire in relating how glad you are to be a part of an obviously outstanding company and a member of a winning team. Don't address your comments solely to CEO. Glance around your audience to project yourself to all as Mr. Regular Sincere Guy or Ms. Pleasant Nice Lady. Don't try to be funny. Save your good lines for other occasions when you can get more mileage out of them.

Lay off the liquor at the cocktail party. The same taboo applies to wine served at a coming-out luncheon. A loose lip can sink your ship before it sets sail.

If you join a company while a cost-cutting binge is under way, you'll be given neither reception nor luncheon. Instead, you will be presented at a meeting of your peers and leading executives.

Whether you are introduced at a reception, luncheon, or meeting, visit briefly with everyone present. The amount of time and attention given each should be based on relative standing in the hierarchy. Say little about yourself. Question all of them about their particular responsibilities to demonstrate your personal interest.

Should your debut consist only of your boss's taking you around the office to meet your peers and those with whom you will be working directly, recognize you are presently regarded as small potatoes. Don't become disheartened or disillusioned, at least not immediately. Accept the fact that you have a lot of role playing to do to improve your position.

If your inauguration consists of your boss's secretary doing the introductions, do not lose your temper. Everyone makes mistakes. Clearly you have made a big one. Start immediately on contacting personnel directors of other companies.

Your welcome can be considered adequate even if you were not presented to all or any of the top executives, but recognize that you must meet them on your own. Create a good reason for introducing yourself to them. Put on a good act, but don't overplay. All you want to do at this point is to let them know who you are and what your present position is. You are seeking coattails sturdy enough to pull you to the top. Try to determine executives with whom you are most likely to develop ties that bind.

If you are among the fortunate few who secured their parts through the good offices of CEO or another top executive, your need for friends stems from an entirely different root. Regardless of the source of the pull which put you where you are—membership in the same club or family connections—play it down. News of the arrival of an anointed one will have spread quickly through the office grapevine, so don't deny the connection. Rather, concentrate on projecting yourself as a nice, regular, extraordinarily talented person who was sought for the position because of outstanding past performance.

Embellish your performance record. Even if your previous company went broke or was on the brink of failing when you left, speak only of your successes. Through skilled role playing you can sell the legend of ability rather than good connections as the reason you were picked for the position.

YOUR OFFICE

Create an atmosphere that suggests to all who enter "Much important business conducted here."

With-it companies allow wide latitude in selecting furniture and decor to fit individual tastes. Those fortunate enough to enjoy such freedom should take full advantage of it in arranging their offices in a style appropriate for the position held. But common sense should be used. Far-out furniture and vivid colors should be avoided.

Yesterday-was-wonderful companies decree both furniture style and color schemes. In many such organizations the decor is early-American yuk. Decorate by the rules, but try to add a frill or two without raising the eyebrows of the highbrows.

Wall hangings and desk decorations reveal a great deal about an individual. Make sure yours proclaim "classy comer."

Diplomas from institutions of higher learning are acceptable wall hangings for those in the moving-up stage. Never are diplomas seen in the offices of top executives, except those of the very few who didn't receive degrees but were given honorary ones in return for generous gifts.

If you attended a six-week course offered by a prestigious business school, you may be strongly tempted to display your certificate of attendance. Keep in mind, though, that those who complete military Officer Candidate Schools in twelve weeks are laughed off as ninety-day wonders. Proclaiming and puffing your attendance may cause you to be accused of being a certified, half-assed, ninety-day wonder. It is permissible, in fact advantageous, to refer to your attending the business school and to drop names of people you met there. But don't mention the length of your stay.

Certificates of successful completion of study courses offered in your particular profession or specialty are acceptable hangings. Those indicating you attended a seminar or conference, completed a correspondence course, or earned some "continuing education credits" are definitely not status builders. A certificate identifying you as a notary public won't add to your prestige but will surely produce a lot of snickers.

Display a family photo provided the kids are under fourteen years of age and the picture is not huge. Creating the impression of strong family ties is useful in projecting the right image. If you have more than three kids, forget the photo. If you are in a second marriage or more, show no family pictures. The Puritan ethic still predominates in most executive suites. Don't give a smart-mouth the opportunity to ask "Which one is this?"

Use caution in displaying awards and citations from service clubs or your alma mater. Use restraint in exhibiting photos which include you. Egotism and self-centeredness are characteristics required of role players. The trick is to be egotistical and self-centered while appearing modest and selfless.

A fancy pen set ranks as a must-have decoration. If you are unfortunate enough to be among the small minority not having one bearing an inscription recognizing your contributions, real or alleged, to some organization or cause, fill the void. Have one engraved, making sure it includes the universal lead "In deep appreciation." Merely "In appreciation" is not enough.

Signs proclaiming a specific philosophy displayed on desks or walls have become quite chic since President Harry S. Truman's "The buck stops here" received so much publicity. Your sign should convey the characteristics required for both your present position and the one you covet. Make sure the printing and the frame are attractive.

To appear thoughtful and inventive, try "There's a better way to do it—find it" by Thomas Edison. Those wanting to be recognized as hard-driving workaholics can use old Tom's "Genius is one percent inspiration and ninety-nine percent perspiration."

Role players may project strong character with the old standby from Shakespeare's Hamlet: "This above all, to thine own self be true." But they should ignore the suggestion. Courage is demonstrated by "In war there is no substitute for victory," advice from General Douglas MacArthur. Since many of the people you are trying to impress probably are MacArthurphiles, this one can be a real winner, especially for those involved in marketing.

Never display quotes from anyone who might be considered anti-business. If the author is unknown, referred to officially as "anonymous," show only the statement.

Possessors of trophies won at golf or tennis tournaments are wise to keep them at home. In their envy the less gifted may label the owners as golf or tennis bums. Owners of bowling trophies should wrap them in opaque paper and seal them in a box in the basement or melt them for scrap.

If your golf or tennis trophy came from winning in a bracket composed of mediocre or poor players, don't display it. As you move up the ladder you may be involved in golf games or tennis matches with the muckety-mucks. If you have billed yourself as a good player and you turn out to be a poor one, the mucks will not be pleased.

Trophy fish and deer or elk heads are gross and have no place in the office. One may be OK for your den, but by all means take it down before a top executive visits your home.

Sell hard to get drapes for your office. Being able to let in or shut out light with one pull of a string is to possess great power. Select only high-quality, solid-color fabrics, preferably soft beige or light tan.

Try to obtain one chair completely different from any other in the company. Refer to it as your "think chair." These two words are more potent than ten thousand pictures.

Never allow a typewriter within your office walls, even in dire emergencies. To type is to brand yourself as a "forever clerk." If you use a dictating machine or calculator, get the pocket-size variety. Acquire a desktop computer as soon as you can.

Phones with lots of lights and push buttons are most impressive. A hold button is an absolute must. So is a buzzer for summoning your secretary.

A speaker phone shouts "I have arrived," making it the ultimate office accoutrement. Coveted by all who aspire to top spots, a speaker phone may not come easily. Keep trying until you get one.

Anyone allowed to choose the color of the telephone should always select red, which connotes both urgency and power.

Do not be deceived by the old canard "An orderly desk indicates an orderly mind." Follow the rule which actually applies: "Behind a cluttered desk is a very busy person." The size of the pile of papers in an office is thought to be directly proportional to the power of the occupant.

Be sure all your desk decorations are currently in vogue. When Richard Nixon was President, his favorite gift to supporters was a golf ball with his signature, mounted on a stand. Once the sight of one evoked oohs and ahs of admiration. Nowadays the few which haven't been thrown into the trash can bring forth groans of disbelief and snide comments. No wonder! Everyone knows Nixon was a lousy golfer.

Desk pieces producing the question "What's that?" enable you to demonstrate that you know more than your inquisitor. Displaying a pyramid with Abraham Maslow's hierarchy of basic needs conveys your deep understanding of human nature. When explaining the meaning of the pyramid to your ignoramus visitor, indicate your surprise, even shock, that anyone with executive responsibilities isn't thoroughly familiar with Maslow's theories, which are the underpinnings of what makes Sammy run.

BOOKS AND MAGAZINES

Deciding which titles to display and which to keep out of sight may be your most important decision in picking your props. Many people associate a book display with the contents of the displayer's mind. Arrange your display to make it appear as if your brain is crammed with intellectual goodies.

Absolutely required are the latest books pertaining to both your line of business and particular specialty. Strictly forbidden are those the slightest bit critical of any business.

Regardless of your particular skills, load up heavily on general business works. The stairway to the top is constructed of that amorphous material known as management skills. One work from the prolific pen of Peter Drucker is a must, two are OK, three a bit much.

Your unfailing devotion to the free enterprise system and conservative economic theory should be displayed publicly. Exhibiting a copy of *Free to Choose* by Milton and Rose Friedman is very effective in conveying your commitment to the cause. Merely seeing the Friedman name twinkles the eyes of any business person deserving of that designation. Books lauding supply-side economics are highly revered.

Keep your book collection current with trends. Add to and delete from the grouping to adapt to changing conditions. In the early Seventies, *Future Shock* was the pièce de résistance in every executive's bookcase. Quite rare in those days was a speech by a CEO which didn't include at least one quote from that book. Some who quoted from it had even read it. Because much of what was once billed as "future shock" has become present reality, the prestige value of the book is now minimal. Make sure a current "in" book, such as *Megatrends,* is prominently displayed.

Agreement with the theories advanced and philosophies espoused by a book is not a requirement for it to be included in your collection. You don't even need to have read it, but it is a good idea to read at least the summary on the inside of the cover just in case questions are asked. The true value of books displayed is determined by impression made rather than information gained.

Women should not display any of the many books now available which offer them advice on how to get ahead in business. To do so risks being judged as not playing by the rules of the company. Follow the valid advice in such books but keep quiet about the source of your guidance.

You will also be judged by the magazines and newspapers you read, or at least display. A recent issue of the *Harvard Business Review* should be exhibited at all times. An absolute must is a copy of the *Wall Street Journal* kept constantly in sight. If you share your copy with others and don't think you can afford your own subscription (how an executive could not afford this esteemed journal of business boggles the mind), keep an old copy on hand. Place it face down so the date can't be noticed.

A copy of *National Review* gives further testimony to your allegiance to conservative political thought as postulated by William F. Buckley, Jr., and friends. Your copy also creates the illusion you understand the big words he and his cohorts are so fond of using.

Fortune is quite acceptable. So is *Business Week. Forbes* is OK, but keep in mind that "After all, a number of the articles are quite critical of some businesses and business leaders."

A dictionary, thesaurus, *Bartlett's Quotations,* vocabulary builder, and similar works may be kept in your office as long as they are out of sight. Accomplished role players don't display any aids which could give the impression they don't carry all the answers in their heads.

Meretricious publications offering to make you a millionaire in three days denote both greed and shallowness. Books advocating positive thinking are acceptable for sales and marketing people but not for aspirants to the executive suite. Such works concentrate on emotion. Management must be concerned with logic.

Finally, as you move up the ladder you will want to add a handsome globe to your office to demonstrate that your view of business is as wide as the world.

CHAPTER 10

ACT LIKE AN EXECUTIVE

From the day you are promoted or join a new company, develop a strategy for impressing and attracting favorable attention from the top executives. Their initial perceptions must be favorable for you to create future opportunities. Determine to get off to a good start.

OFFICE HOURS

Many companies now use the LIFO (last in—first out) method of inventory accounting. Role players should adopt the FILO (first in—last out) system of office hours.

Arrive at least fifteen, preferably thirty, minutes before your peers and superiors. Being first in will not be easy, unless you are a hopeless insomniac. Other role players also understand that in the eyes of those who matter, the amount of time spent in the office seems to count for far more than what is accomplished in the office.

If you can't be first in without losing too much sleep (turning in a top performance day after day requires a high energy level), settle for second or even third. But be there long before the official starting time.

Upon arrival, always close your office door. Curiosity about your reasons for shutting off the outside world will quickly reach fever pitch. "What the hell is going on in there?" will be on everyone's lips. Eventually someone will call up the courage to ask you: "Why do you shut your door every morning?" Affix a "doesn't everyone" look on your face and answer, "Simple. To plan my day and establish priorities." No further questions will be asked.

What you actually do behind the closed door is your business. But just don't sit there drinking coffee. If you read the newspaper, stash it in your briefcase, for while you are at lunch your wastebasket will be checked for newspapers and cups.

Keep on your desk a columnar pad with lots of lines and notations. Refer to it only as "my plans." A multi-page computer printout provides another useful safety valve.

One happening that you can count on with certainty is that sooner or later, probably sooner, curiosity about "what is really going on in there" will be so overwhelming that someone will muster up the temerity to crash the scene. The sudden click of the door handle may or may not be preceded by a knock. When the crasher comes, always be prepared to be pondering your pad or computer printout with pencil in hand. Stare briefly at the pad or printout, then look up and in a calm, but distinctly cool tone say "Yes." After the "pardon me's" have been stammered out, walk the intruder to the door, then close the door but don't slam it. Soon the grapevine will spread the word that you really are working behind the closed door.

If any of your subordinates have offices, you can be certain they, too, will close their doors upon arrival. Only after they have heard yours click will theirs open.

Two basic rules apply to the timing of opening your door: one, only after your boss has arrived; two, at varied times, rather than always at the same time. Never be predictable. If you have had a tough night you can keep your door closed until you have shaken the cobwebs.

Inevitably, you will be assigned a special project which will have a significant bearing on your future prospects. When your turn comes, keep the door closed all day to demonstrate to one and all the great importance of your assignment. Open your door occasionally to ask your secretary for a file. Wait for it, then close the door. At closing time, open the door, say good night to the troops, then close the door. By these gestures you make it clear that those destined for top spots never rest and that your diligence and dedication set you apart from the slovenly slobs who keep "post office hours."

Linger in the evening at least an hour after closing time. Never look up from your desk when you suspect one of the major domos is making le grand tour to determine those working or at least still on the premises. Reach immediately for the columnar pad or computer printout. Pick up your pencil, assume a contemplative pose, and wait. If he wants to talk he'll come in. But he'll know you are there and will certainly let your boss know how impressed he is with your exemplary work habits.

Those who would be big successes must clearly recognize the promotion possibilities inherent merely in arriving early and staying late. You must consistently come early and stay late. Just sometimes won't cut it. Many CEOs seem to place an inordinate amount of importance on the arrival and departure habits of would-be executives. That some do not attach the same significance to their own arrival or departure times is apparently not relevant.

What you do in the after hours is not important, except that you always appear to be engrossed in serious business when CEO or another top executive is near. You can pay your bills, handle personal correspondence, or use the company's WATS line to talk to out-of-town relatives and friends.

When you leave early, as sometimes you must, depart several hours before closing time. Because you are known as a stay-late, it will be assumed you are on your way to an important business meeting. Say nothing to shatter the illusion. Always take your briefcase with you on early departures, even if you are going to the dentist and had to admit it. Give the impression you will be working while you wait.

ACTING IMPORTANT

You will not always be busy, but you must always appear to be busy.

Keep a planning book with you at all times which enables you to allocate each hour of your working day. When asked about your availability at a certain time, always check your planner before giving your answer. When scheduling the next meeting of subordinates, make a big deal out of reviewing your planner before announcing the time and date. Set a time limit on the meeting to emphasize your heavy schedule.

Be quite slow about returning internal phone calls from peers and even slower in calling back subordinates. Never apologize for being a bit dilatory. Be very prompt in returning calls of superiors.

When a peer or subordinate phones for an appointment, always be too busy to grant an immediate audience. The longer you delay, the busier you appear to be.

Make sure your secretary answers all your phone calls. It is not only inefficient for an executive to answer the phone, it is also unseemly. It is OK to instruct your secretary to ask "Who is calling, please?" if you also inform her to make sure she doesn't give that line to your boss or a top executive.

Your secretary may initiate phone calls in situations you control, such as to subordinates and suppliers. "Mary from Mr. or Ms. Eager's office—please hold for Mr. or Ms. Eager" demonstrates real power to the people you control. People who control you, superiors and customers, may think their time is as valuable as yours and hang up on Mary.

Always keep a copy of your strategic operational plan in your pocket secretary. When a superior asks about the progress of a particular project, pull out your plan sheet and answer, "Let's see where that one prioritizes."

Each word you speak or write to your boss should clearly convey the message "I am a team player, and I am doing and will continue to do all I can to help you win, captain."

How best to convey this vital message depends upon the circumstances of your promotion or hiring. If your boss selected you from a group of applicants, you won't have much convincing to do. Everyone wants to be right, especially those who refer to themselves, in tones dripping with pride, as leaders. If you don't screw up ridiculously, the boss is sure to believe your message.

Bosses are not noted for their altruism. You were hired to make the boss look good. Accomplishing this mission will sometimes require your making yourself look stupid, a practice known as incurring short-term losses in order to reap long-term rewards.

If the boss hired you to solve a particular problem, talk about it as much as possible, but always call it "*our* problem."

In developing the demanded instant solution, employ one of the key principles of role playing: disguise activity as usefulness. Inundate the boss with reports and analyses. Hold many meetings on the subject. Keep your office door closed at all times—no exceptions. Have your dinner sent in at least three times a week. Phone a lot of out-of-town experts, then flood the boss with numerous memos on the conversations.

Wear no suit jacket or blazer during the crisis. The boss will surely be impressed with your "coats off to the future" dedication.

Convey the impression that you are thinking about *our problem* twenty-four hours a day. Mention that a great idea occurred to you during the night, so you got up and put it on paper. Then read the great idea to your boss.

What about solving the problem? Keep on writing reports, conducting studies, and talking with experts. Under no circumstances, including a direct request from the boss, should you submit a specific recommended solution. If such a solution doesn't work, and it probably won't, your neck will be in the noose.

"Covering your ass" is an important aspect of role playing. Submit all your suggestions in bits and pieces, always including a number of suggested approaches, but never "the solution." When your boss selects one of the possibilities you suggested, it becomes "his plan."

Use generous amounts of "on the other hand," "perhaps," "alternatively," and other slippery terms to make it difficult, preferably impossible, to develop your ideas into a specific plan. Never be sucked into creating a number of scenarios so that all probable contingencies will be covered. Talking about scenarios is a big part of role playing. Restrain your interest in scenarios until you are in a position to request them from subordinates.

Problems have a way of solving themselves if nature and other forces at work are allowed to take their course. Time solves tough problems more effectively than do specific plans, even strategic plans. The problem will go away or the company will fold. Accept the fact that you really have no control over which of the two will occur. Instead, concentrate on your act of disguising activity as usefulness.

Making the boss look good. Your present mission is to please the boss at all times. The easiest way to accomplish this aim is to make the boss look good. Sometimes, perhaps often, that will not be easy to do. Your task will be especially troublesome if your boss possesses that most lethal of all weapons, the jawbone of an ass.

To help cope with trying situations the boss has created with his or her mouth, be prepared to be a walking apologia. Develop an arsenal of explanations for faux pas: "You misunderstood"; "You are confused on that one"; "That was a joke; don't you appreciate a sense of humor?"

Avoid being cozy with any of the boss's superiors or peers, especially if the crown lies uneasily on the head. The more incompetent the boss is, the more likely it is you are working for an accomplished role player. Proficient role players suffer frequently from acute paranoia. When any top executive praises you, a paranoid boss may suspect you of being a conspirator planning an overthrow.

Your objective is to become the boss's favorite underling. Even if the boss is totally unbearable, a complete unadulterated jerk, suffer the fool in silence until you are firmly established. Then you can start undercutting.

If you were hired by your boss's boss, you need to put on an entirely different act. You can be certain your boss is not jumping with joy over the fact that you are in the cast through a higher power. If you are wired into the top, who will keep you from getting your boss's role? The boss will.

Base your act on the strength of your ties to the top. If they are truly strong, patronize the boss until the inevitable day comes when you are given his or her job or a better one. If ties are flimsy, if the one who put you in your present role doesn't give a damn where you end up, you have a serious problem.

A flimsy tie to the top will require your using to the fullest all your acting skills. You must break your ass (figuratively, of course) to display your unstinting loyalty and dedication to the boss. This act will be much harder to pull off than it would be if the boss had hired you.

Be aware of the possibility—a quite strong one in a closely held company—that your boss is a fellow club member or family friend of CEO or a leading light. Never refer to the boss's ties to the top.

When the boss mentions inside connections, and it will probably be in a self-deprecating way, ignore the comment. Above all, don't agree with it. Maintain a deadpan expression on your face lest it flash "You're damn right." Chuckle a bit out of respect to the boss's truly charming sense of humor, then move quickly to another subject.

THE COMPANY'S LANGUAGE

All companies have developed an indigenous jargon. Most have created a hybrid variety by mixing accepted industry lingo with esoteric terminology coined by past and present top executives.

Company terminology is so sacred to leading lights that violations are regarded as capital sins. Learn the language of your company and begin using it as quickly as you can.

How rapidly you learn to use the argot effectively is directly related, to a surprising extent, to your rate of progress.

Two old faithful words, "employee" and "salesman," demonstrate the dynamics of business language. Everyone knows that these words mean "one who works for wages"; and "one who sells a product or service." Now, however, in many companies an employee is an "associate" and a salesman a "sales consultant" or "representative."

Learn both the proper usage and pronunciation of each word or phrase comprising the jargon. In some companies and industries, the frequently used inside terms may be so obscure that pronouncing them as they sound can be quite risky. In keeping with role playing's underlying philosophy of always playing it safe, don't use any words you have not heard a top executive speak. Then, and only then, can you be certain of correct pronunciation and usage. Never depend on a clerical type to use or pronounce a word correctly.

You must also learn and use the "in" words popular with those in the executive suite. "In" words are best described as those which masquerade as contributions to thought. To know and to use them at the right place and time proves that you know what turns on the powerhouse.

Learn CEO's favorite words and phrases. Give first priority to this task. Initially, your monitoring of these words of wisdom will consist of your reading and rereading written words, as your personal contacts will be few. When you encounter him personally you will be too preoccupied with making a favorable impression on him to hear a word he says.

Closely auditing CEO's words must be an ongoing process. Each of the pronouncements emanating from Mount Sinai should be scrutinized closely for patterns of word usage. Write down words or phrases which keep reappearing. Always use them as he does, never to convey the dictionary definition.

When CEO gives a speech, listen with notebook in hand. Extemporaneous talks are best for providing clues to his favorites. His formal talks and written communications are probably prepared by his ghost writers, but it is unlikely there is a big difference. If the writers don't sprinkle the scripts with big doses of his favorite words, phrases, and cliches, they won't be CEO's writers for very long.

An excellent way to get a head start on learning and using words popular with Top Star and other leading lights is to read Edwin Newman's books, *A Civil Tongue* and *Strictly Speaking—Will America Be the Death of English.* Each includes numerous examples of words and expressions which do violence to the language. List each one. Chances are good that each one originated in business and is currently enjoying great popularity in many companies. Most top executives are not renowned for their study of, or interest in, proper English usage.

Use buzz words. Those used universally in all types of companies and industries.

There seems to be no middle ground in regard to the acceptance of "wise" after a noun—strategywise, saleswise, approachwise. Most companies either warmly embrace the practice or totally ban it. Determining immediately whether "wise" is in or out at your company is a prudent step—role playingwise.

Using nouns as verbs is heady stuff at practically all companies. Don't tell your boss you will send him a memo. Say "I'll memo you on that." President Reagan gave us a new one: "Round table it."

Two words CEO and Number Two (probably Numbers Three through Fourteen, too) relish applying to their operations are "integrity" and "character." No decision, regardless of how self-serving, cannot be justified by cloaking it in either of these two words.

Situation A: The sales force complains that the product is inferior to the competition's, over-priced, and out of date. Response to A: "The integrity of this company has been developed over decades of unceasing effort and dedication to serving the needs of our customers. We shall not allow a passing fad to destroy our integrity."

Situation B: Earnings continue to fall quarter after quarter. Response to B: "The character of a company, as demonstrated by long-term performance, is a much more valid criterion of appraisal than the quantity of short-term results."

Use "character" and "integrity" frequently when rationalizing unpopular decisions or trying to justify unwise ones.

Using acronyms is always an acceptable, and frequently applaudable act. Accomplished role players never refer to the Economic Recovery Tax Act of 1981 by its name, nor do they even use the initials. They use it as a word: er' ta. They do the same with the Tax Equity and Fiscal Responsibility Act of 1982, calling it tef' ra. You should, too. Management by objective, an operating philosophy espoused by practically all companies but actually practiced by few, should always be referred to as MBO.

"Feedback," "input," and "output" are standard lines in every company and industry. "Interim evaluation wave," however, impresses only top role players in such businesses as advertising and market research.

Quite a few use management by metaphor or simile: "This assignment is a piece of cake"; "Selling our super-duper special is like shooting fish in a barrel"; and that horror of horrors, "The greatest thing since sliced bread."

Do not mistake big words for "in" words. As a general rule, most top executives avoid using big words to demonstrate they are communicating effectively with the great unwashed. Exceptions to this rule come in two categories: those who really know the English language and love to throw big words around, and the insecure who use vocabulary books or collect jawbreakers from William F. Buckley, Jr.'s columns. The first group is rare, the second more common. If you work for category one, don't use a big word unless it slides off your tongue smoothly or adds pizzazz to a written sentence. If you work for category two, follow the act.

Go easy on jock jargon. Some, but not many, companies are big on using sports terminology. Companies in which jock jargon holds sway do not face problems—they are confronted with a second and fifteen. Confidence in reaching an objective is expressed as "That's just a soft wedge." A goof is passed off with "I fumbled that one."

Leaders in jock jargon companies frequently refer to themselves as "coach." Their memos to the troops may sometimes include their headshot superimposed on a muscular body wearing a T-shirt with "Coach" on the front and a whistle around the neck. Only role players with tremendous egos and thick skins should attempt this act.

A non-jock associated with a company at which the sports section of the paper takes precedence over the *Wall Street Journal* has a gigantic problem. The only possible hope of coping lies in buying a book of sports terminology and memorizing the contents.

If sports terms aren't in vogue in your company, and they are not in most, don't use any. You may think you are guided by Divine Providence when you describe a plan you have developed as one "which plays on the field as well as it diagrams on the blackboard," but a non-jock boss will surely give you a stare flashing: "Just what in the hell are you trying to say?"

Keep selling yourself. Each moment you are under the eyes of higher-ups your actions are being scrutinized and your future potential evaluated. Make sure your every action impresses observers and your demeanor radiates executive ability. Constantly acting like an executive is the single most important aspect of effective self-promotion. Initially, then, before going to the office each morning go to a mirror, look yourself squarely in the eye and say in a firm, persuasive tone: "I really am an executive—I really am." Within six months or so you will have convinced yourself and those people watching you that you really are.

CHAPTER 11

STUDY YOUR COMPETITION

As quickly as you can, determine who is in and who is out at your company. Recognize that outs never return as ins. They are always ignored and left "to twist slowly, slowly in the wind." Once you have identified an out, shun him.

First spot the ins among your peers. Thoroughly analyze each to determine weaknesses and strengths. Your goal is to find the best ways of calling attention to weaknesses and deemphasizing strengths. Yes, that is your aim. You are not involved in a laughter-filled taffy pull. If you seek to move on to a top spot, you must put footprints on the backs of your rivals.

Understand that both superior and peer ins can suddenly become outs, even overnight, and that new ins, at least potential ones, will be hired from time to time. Keep current your list of ins and outs.

Here are some typical ins you will find among your peer

group and the next higher level and suggested ways to make them outs.

THE FAIR-HAIRED BOY

Your boss's number-one man is the major roadblock in your career path. Sight in on him from the day you join the show, but don't pull the trigger until you are confident you can wipe him out with a direct hit. Merely wounding him is not enough.

Discover the real, as distinct from alleged, function he performs. If, as is the case with many Fair Haireds, he is merely a conduit of gossip and grumblings picked from the grapevine, he's a sitting duck. You'll have no big problem getting him out of your way. When he pumps for information, give it to him gladly. Just make sure that everything you tell him is inaccurate. Anyone misinforming the boss won't be an in for very long.

If telling tales isn't his act, chances are he's a doer—one who completes each assignment correctly and quickly. He is very conscientious, ambitious, but not too—more of a follower than a leader. In short, he is a lousy role player. Let the boss's light shine upon him. He's never going to make it to the top. He was born to sit behind an "assistant to" nameplate.

Keep in mind, however, that "assistant to" types are frequently gripped by fright when bright newcomers appear on the scene. Their fear stems, not from concern about somebody passing them up, but rather from dread that the new boss will hire a new "assistant to." Not only are "assistants to" nervous nellies, they are usually nit-picky and complete bores. Expect him to nit-pick your act, but don't lose any sleep worrying about the results of his efforts.

Tell your boss what a great detail man "assistant to" is—a way of damning with faint praise—and keep requesting his indispensable services on important projects. Keeping him bogged down in details keeps him out of your hair.

If Fair Haired is not a pipeline or doer, recognize that you have a serious problem. For in all likelihood he is an accomplished role player who has set his sights on getting the boss's job. You must beat him at his own act or find a new company.

THE FAIR-HAIRED WOMAN

She's bright, articulate, and determined to make it to the top. She holds an MBA from a prestigious school. She's respected throughout the company and is becoming well known in her industry.

FHW is neither a pipeline to the boss nor an "assistant to." Rather, she runs her own operation and runs it well. A number of men report to her. She and CEO are on a first-name basis.

An ideal combination of feminine charm and a businesslike approach, she is neither fox nor shrinking violet. Her family credentials are impeccable—her husband is a partner in a prominent law firm and her two children attend a fancy private school.

In meetings, FHW remains silent until she has something to say, then says it precisely and properly. Her manner is charming, in fact disarming. But male rivals have learned to their lasting regret that she is expert at tossing barbs without losing her composure. Those trying to put her down usually end up with egg on their faces. She is particularly adept at ripping apart stupid statements.

FHW has spoken publicly on a number of issues affecting her company and industry, but she is much too smart and ambitious to limit her statements to "women's issues." Her eyes are always on the big picture.

Women role players should attempt to hitch to her star, hoping she'll pull them along with her on her inevitable march to the ranks of top executives. Men can only hope that another company will make FHW an offer she can't refuse.

THE ANALYZER

An expert on everybody else's job, he expresses no opinions before the fact. After the deed is done, he knows exactly how it *should* have been done. He examines the remains of a failed project with the thoroughness of a coroner at an inquest. He doesn't make constructive suggestions; rather, he picks the fly specks out of the pepper.

Never does he make a statement without leaving a loophole through which he can crawl out to proclaim "I told you so." Watch the sneaky bastard at all times.

Analyzer does not look like a role player. On him expensive suits look cheap. His word rate is deliberate, as if sifted through a sieve before crossing his lips. He has the wet look, each hair firmly pasted to his skull.

Never underestimate Analyzer by dismissing him as a mere bean counter. He is quite ambitious, harboring both the hope and belief that he will become a top executive.

Analyzer loves to talk about getting things done, but somehow gets by dissecting the results of what others have done. He avoids making decisions because he knows that not making any is safer.

There is only one way to remove Analyzer from your path—maneuver him out of the role he plays so well into one he can't handle. When a project comes along that excites the leading players, use all your persuasive powers to convince the one who makes the decision that Analyzer is the logical choice for project leader.

Anyone as disingenuous as Analyzer is not going to be outflanked easily. He will do his best to avoid being stuck with specific accountability. When the name for another project leader is discussed, play up that one's weaknesses and cite Analyzer's strengths.

Once Analyzer is put in charge of the project, you can strike his name from the list of ins. He'll become so bogged down in details and accumulate so much worthless information that he'll never meet his deadline.

GREAT I AM

Most companies of any size have at least one GIA. Every other word he utters is I. Practically every happening reminds him of a personal experience. Frequently he is a specialist or technician who has done an above-average job.

As the years passed, his ego fed upon itself until it became so bloated that now it obscures his other qualities.

GIA has long since quit acting as if he does any work. He is totally absorbed in acting important—really important. He's an in rapidly on the way to becoming an out—and is the only one who doesn't know it. In the words of Graham Greene: "A dying flame looks as if it has never been anything but smoke."

GIA constantly talks about the many wonderful deeds he has performed for the company. Completely devoid of perspective, he regards every hill as Mount Everest. GIA is as quick to criticize both superiors and peers (although he finds it quite difficult to conceive of anyone being his equal, let alone his better) as he is to praise himself. His nagging insecurities compel him to build himself up by tearing others down.

At first meeting, GIA will probably come across as charming, intelligent, and, of course, quite important. To add to his sense of importance, he seeks to develop a band of faithful followers. Newcomers to the executive ranks are especially sought after as disciples.

Humor GIA, but never take him seriously. Under no circumstances confide in him or seek his support. Associating with him will not only jeopardize your future, but also bore the hell out of you. His tales are far from charming upon the fifth or sixth hearing.

You need take no action to solve the problems created by GIA's presence. Eventually, CEO will call up the courage to remove him.

BOOKWORM

By his high forehead, thick glasses, drab attire, and large Adam's apple you can spot Bookworm. As you check his tacky appearance, chances are quite good that you will spot a Phi Beta Kappa key hanging somewhere.

Bookworm has few redeeming qualities. He is as athletic as a two-legged elephant. He has read most of the literature on his particular specialty, but very little on any other subject. His written communications are so heavily laden with technical terms and pedantic posturings they are unintelligible. His feet are planted firmly in mid-air, enabling him to come down on the side of the leading lights. His pseudo-Socratic approach of responding to a question by asking another one is a carefully contrived technique to cover up his single-track intelligence.

As Worm is indisputably an All-American jerk, you can write him off immediately, right? Wrong! Because of his exceptional grade-point average, Worm was hired to perform as the company's intellectual. And he plays that role to the hilt.

Worm's mind is a veritable storehouse of technical information. Since coming aboard, he has passed all study courses offered in his specialty in record time and with high honors. Early in life he learned that the grades earned in acquiring knowledge count for much more than how effectively that knowledge is used. He is very aware of, and comfortable with, his role of local brain. Every night before retiring he kisses the copy of his college transcripts, which he keeps under his pillow.

Worm can be handled, but putting him away will take a long time and lots of chutzpah. If he is not a direct roadblock, avoid confrontation in the hope you can skirt around him. But if he is or likely will be in your way, remove him you must.

Go to work on his weakness—lack of knowledge of areas other than his own. Get him on your ground, far away from the comfort and security of his own territory.

Oscar Wilde wrote "Caricature is the tribute that mediocrity pays to genius." Caricature Worm at every opportunity, but don't appear mediocre in the process. When he makes a stupid statement on a subject you know and he doesn't, magnify his flub. Cut him hard—but only in the presence of peers. Top executives become quite upset when someone laughs at their brain.

Soon your peers, as frustrated as you by Worm's preeminence, will join you in caricaturing his one-dimensional intelligence. As more and more of the middle managers begin to regard Worm as a subject of ridicule rather than adulation, the leaders will first wonder, then start to worry about Worm. In time, Worm will be given a special assignment. Then he is finished as a foe.

WELL CREDENTIALED

If it is your unfortunate fate to be competing with someone tied closely to CEO through family connections, membership in The Country Club, or same social circle, mark him for special handling or be prepared to move on quickly. To attempt to compete with a Well Credentialed on the basis of skills or to try to out-role play him is to commit the business equivalent of self-immolation.

Chances are good that a Well Credentialed exists in your midst. Uncover him as quickly as you can. Immediately suspect those with II or III behind their names. Another clue is a middle name that is also a surname. If that name is that of a now- or once-prominent local family, it's likely you have uncovered a Well Credentialed. Fabricate an excuse to borrow the biographies of all executives to learn who belongs to the same country club as CEO. When you find one, you have found your Well Credentialed. When you see an underling talking to CEO as if he were a peer, you have also uncovered a Well Credentialed.

Another way of detecting wires to the top is to check the past success patterns of those seemingly on the rise. Anyone with a lackluster record of progress at a previous company who now ranks among the chosen few after only a short association should be watched carefully.

Once you have found a Well Credentialed, handle him very carefully, especially if his close ties to the top derive from common social standing. His preoccupation with appearances stems from the intensive peer pressure to which he is subjected. His fellow socialites bombard him constantly with tales of their travels and weekend excursions. He, in turn, must have some exciting and glamorous stories to tell them.

Reconcile yourself to the fact that Well Credentialed's fate is out of your hands. You will not be able to get him out of your way. Taking potshots at him will only precipitate your downfall. All you can hope for is that someone near the top will feel so threatened by Well Credentialed's presence that he will try to get him out of his way. Not only should you hope a higher-up will take him on, you should also supply him with ammunition for his attack. But don't let CEO catch you doing it.

Although the vast majority of Well Credentialeds are men, don't overlook the possibility of a woman falling into that category. A daughter of CEO's wife's college roommate can progress very rapidly.

BULLY

Cocksure and aggressive, Bully is macho man personified. He firmly clings to and faithfully practices the tenet that making a lot of noise equates with having a lot of power. It is unlikely that Bully has read *Success Through Intimidation;* most Bullies regard reading as a sissy's sport. But he could surely write a stirring dissertation on the same subject based on his experiences.

Bully is above average in intelligence, but no genius. He is so intractable in his opinions (he has one on every subject) and so forceful in expressing them that the leading players regard him as super smart. Thus a mutually satisfying situation is created: top executives are spared the ordeal of confronting him; Bully is quite willing to carry their spears.

Usually Bully is physically imposing, appearing as formidable as he acts. Bully feasts on the soft-spoken and diffident. He reaches peak form in a crowd when he can interrupt with a comment such as, "If that's the way you think, no wonder your operation is in such a goddamned mess." Clean of speech Bully is not.

Bully charges blithely ahead, stomping on the weak and standing up to the strong. In the process, Bully has developed a potent power base, one not even an accomplished role player should attempt to short-circuit.

Be aware that Bully regards new, ambitious up-and-comers as a special delicacy. He truly loves to devour them. Stay as far away from him as you can, but don't try to hide.

Avoid giving Bully an excuse for unleashing his scythelike tongue on you. Do not deceive yourself into thinking that you have been called by God to bring him to heel. You haven't and you won't.

Accept the fact that Bully is going to be around for a long time because "we need someone like him to keep people on their toes." Your best hope is to move ahead of Bully. Then you can use him as a battering ram to clear the way for you.

RISING STAR

Out of a prestigious firm Rising came, hired to assume an important role. Nattily attired and glib of tongue, Rising is performing his role in such outstanding fashion that he is receiving rave reviews from the top brass. Already they assume that he will soon be one of them.

Rising's eyes have been fixed firmly on stardom since he left his small town to attend the state university. He made good grades, belonged to a prestigious fraternity, and developed many good contacts. In no time at all he was passing as a full-fledged sophisticate. He married well, if money is an appropriate measure of "well." In his previous positions he attracted favorable attention and made impressive friends. He has made good use of them in advancing his career.

Forceful and confident, Rising may not always be right, but he is never in doubt. Unlike Bully, he is suave, rather than belligerent. His office is arranged to depict efficiency and lots of activity. Most comfortable with fast trackers, Rising has little time for lesser lights. Rising doesn't hesitate to drive his car into a crowded intersection or park in places reserved for the handicapped.

A master of moods, Rising knows when to be tough and when to extend the olive branch, when to move and when to hesitate. He has produced some terrific results since joining the company, and unabashedly spreads the word about his feats.

You have but one choice with Rising: make him a meteor or you'll forever be under his influence. You are not alone in your plight; other role players feel the same pressure from his presence. They, too, seek relief from the frightening thought that Rising may become their boss. Unite your fellow sufferers in a cabal against Rising.

Very likely Rising is a master of focusing attention on his triumphs and covering up his debacles. He may be so proficient at the latter that his disasters may be hard to find. He has had some. Keep digging until you have uncovered a good supply.

Rising is very expansive when his deals are going well, but withdrawn, sullen, and defensive when one of his brain children turns out to be defective. Keep him withdrawn and sullen as much as you can. Ask him pointed questions about his projects which have soured. The more you and your partners in the cabal needle him in public, the more defensive he will become. And the more he is on the defensive, the less time he will have to work on productive deals.

Do your part, on the sly of course, about spreading the word about Rising's failings. When his panache begins to pale you'll know he is at least wounded.

Rising will end up in one of two ways: either he will be judged a fraud for covering up his disasters or he will fend off attacks and remain in favor—and you'll be in deep trouble.

MS. NO NONSENSE

She knows her role, knows that she knows it, and doesn't feel the need nor have the desire to impress anyone. She's a poor role player, but one smart cookie.

Ms. No moved into the executive ranks by outperforming a number of would-be male rivals. She's not a female version of Bully, but she doesn't use euphemisms in her speech. To her a stupid idea isn't one that needs more study; it is a stupid idea. When a male peer or superior patronizes her, she doesn't wilt or pout. She tells him to go to hell.

She isn't married, but not because she is unattractive or hasn't been asked. She joined the firm out of college, became career-oriented, working long and hard, and produced outstanding results. She began moving to responsible positions when such recognition for women was rare.

To put it mildly, Ms. No is not the most popular executive in the company. Some men, and a couple of women, have tried to push her into the background, and most have damaged themselves in the process. CEO respects her ability, although he is not enthralled with her attitude, but sometimes contacts her directly for an opinion on a subject related to her specialty. He has considered promoting her to a top spot, but backed off from fear of a major mutiny.

Those working for Ms. No have no problem—as long as they do their work well. It is her peers and superiors who try "to put her in her place" who end up with mud on their faces.

Don't mess with Ms. No. Learn as much about the company's operations as you can from her. But don't try to finesse her lest your career turn out to be a short and unpleasant one.

Above all, don't waste your time trying to pump her about company politics. Ms. No doesn't mess with that stuff. She doesn't need to. What you should strive for in your relationship with Ms. No is peaceful coexistence.

MR. NICE GUY

Nice is both difficult to figure out and very tough to get out of the way. Upon meeting him your first reaction will probably be: "No one is this nice. The son of a bitch has got to be faking." The truth is, he really is a nice guy, and he is not faking.

Nice works very hard, spending long hours actually working rather than trying to impress. He doesn't say a bad word about anyone, not even those who really deserve badmouthing.

He is direct and scrupulously fair, honest, and straight in his dealings with subordinates and superiors, and free of sophistry. People instinctively like Nice, so he has developed a large band of faithful followers and ardent boosters. Although quite ambitious, Nice would never think of helping himself by hurting someone else. A show picking Nice as CEO could do a hell of a lot worse.

But life in the business world being what it is, Nice's chances of becoming CEO are rather remote. Probably a top executive already has him targeted. Rivals are especially wary of popular guys with large followings.

Nice makes an easy target. His foes will hit him hard and frequently, tagging him as too soft or "not tough enough, and by God you gotta be tough to run a department." Chances are, Nice will end up in a pretty high position, so butter him up a bit as you move along.

THE POLITICIAN

A big smile, firm handshake, ebullience, and abundant self-confidence are his trademarks. He seems to have been born with a built-in wind checker, intuitively knowing what stand to take on each issue to end up on the side of the angels.

Epitomizing the superb role player, Pol speaks rapidly and very self-assuredly. Usually he has the answer before the question is asked. Humility is not one of his vices. He vigorously proclaims his accomplishments and importance. So convincing is he that the leading lights have bought the product he sells so enthusiastically—himself.

Although far from being an intellectual, Pol is plenty tricky. By no means is he a slave to the truth. He is a master at putting peers and subordinates in their places, as he sees their places, with cutting remarks all said with a grin which flashes "Of course, I am only kidding."

Setting Pol apart is his uncanny ability to endear himself to all the top executives in spite of their rivalries. A fondness for Pol may be their only common interest. Perhaps that results from Pol's agreeing with their every word in such a way that no one would think of dismissing him as a mere yes man.

Pol knows how to handle every situation. When he is with leading lights who like to party, Pol is first to belly up to the bar and usually the last to leave. When the occasion calls for solemnity and propriety, count on Pol to be solemn and proper. When a meeting becomes tense and anxiety fills the air, Pol will tell a story which makes everyone smile.

To disparage Pol is akin to defacing the American flag. Always praise him to the higher-ups.

What can a red-blooded role player do about handling anyone as clever and slippery as Pol? Not much, except be patient. Pol's charm and cunning will win him promotions—top executive is even a possibility. Eventually he will reach a level where his incompetence is so glaring that he will have to be put out to pasture. In the meantime, enjoy his humor and quick wit.

CHAPTER 12

ATTRACT ATTENTION WITH YOUR MEMOS

Speaking effectively and impressively is very important, but it is not enough to pull you to the top. You also must dazzle top executives—especially Number One—with your ability to put words on paper in a manner which clearly proclaims you as a comer. Your medium for creating this essential image is the office memo.

First, then, understand that the real purpose of a memo is to impress rather than to inform; to further the career of the writer rather than to enlighten the reader. Before beginning a memo to be seen by a higher-up, psych yourself into believing that this particular memo can catapult you to the top. If you persist in maintaining this positive mental attitude, known in the trade as PMA, someday you *will* be right.

Make your memos stand out from the pack. Your rivals probably use standard, company-issue 8½-by-11 or

5-by-8 white bond for their memos. Instead, you should buy high-quality beige or light-green stock, size 7½ by 10 or 4 by 7.

Work hard on making the contents as eye-catching as possible. Don't always use the paragraph form. Gussy up the memo with headlines and subheads, and list your major points in tabular form. Sprinkle liberally with <u>underlines</u>.

Most memo writers have their names typed at the end of the missive. A few bolder souls sign their names above the typed one but, alas, they use pedestrian black or blue ink. Have your name typed, then sign only the first initial of your first name in green ink. Sign it with a flourish. Use only green. Red and purple are too gaudy.

Each memo must have a mission. A memo should impress the reader, but keep in mind that you have three different sets of readers and you need to impress each one differently:

- *Your subordinates*—You call all the shots, and those who behave themselves will be provided for nicely and those who misbehave will be punished severely.
- *Your peers*—You are a competent, nice, warm-hearted team player who wants to do the best possible job for the company and cooperate with all associates, one who would never think of trying to undercut them.
- *Your superiors*—You are one smart cookie, know how and are eager to crack the tough nuts, understand the big picture in the company, and are ready right now for more responsibility (and more pay and perks).

Here are examples of how to use a memo to convey the desired message to each audience:

Situation: You have fired a manager of an operation who was quite popular with the hired help. The natives are restless, consumed with concern about their futures and curiosity about who will be picked to fill the position and the politics involved in the picking. Many people in that department and others in the company think they deserve the prize. Tongues are wagging, rumors are flying, bad feelings are flaring. Everyone is too involved in the new-boss hassle to do any work.

Mission of your memo:

- Calm the churning seas of discontent. Assure everyone that your steady hand at the helm will bring them through the storm.
- Convey the messages: "Don't pout if you aren't picked." "Relax, you're in good hands—mine. So get your asses back to work."

Your memo:

To all the Happy Help:

This memo updates you on developments related to the recently announced organizational restructuring [never say termination] in your department. As you know, I am a firm believer in communicating frankly and fully on vital matters.

Information on any individual believed to be qualified and who has expressed interest in this position will be secured by the professional recruiters I have retained. Employing this method reflects our determination to evaluate a large number of qualified applicants and thereby select <u>the</u> most qualified individual for this important responsibility.

In keeping with the company's long-standing and historically efficacious practice of promoting from within whenever the best candidate is available internally, I hope that someone presently associated with the company emerges from the selection process as the most qualified. I will visit personally with <u>all</u> those passing the preliminary screening and select the one I regard as the most likely to do the outstanding job that I want done.

In addition to stated education and work experience requirements, some basic personal characteristics are also absolutely necessary. These include integrity; character; high intelligence level; high energy level; positive mental attitude.

I am inclined to believe you are reassured of the effectiveness of the selection process by the fact that it is being directed by someone thoroughly familiar with the operation and what it takes to lead it successfully. I know I can count on your one hundred percent cooperation in this important undertaking.

I. M. Incharge
[Sign I with flourish in green ink]

Situation: A peer, one of your keenest rivals for the promotion you covet, requests ideas from you and others on your level on how to develop more business from present customers.

Mission of your memo:

- Avoid giving the ambitious bastard a single idea he can use because more sales to present customers means greater recognition and prestige for him with the hotshots, increasing his chances of getting the promotion you want.
- Give the impression you applaud his ingenuity.
- Express deep regret at being unable to help.

Your memo:

Mr. U. R. Pushy:

What a great idea you have in attempting to develop more business from present customers. Day in and day out we beat our brains trying to uncover new customers and blithely ignoring those who know from experience what a fine company we are and what good products we sell. Congratulations on using the old bean to come up with a gem.

Curses! Your request comes when I am up to my armpits in the many activities associated with

Operation Mother Lode (OML). As you know, we're swinging the pick day and night to be sure we hit the big strike. When this important mission is accomplished I will check back with you to see if my thoughts on this subject can still be useful.

I. M. Cagey
[Sign I with flourish in green ink]

Situation: While reading the latest edition of the company magazine during an attack of dyspepsia, Big Boss becomes convinced communications with associates are atrocious and directly responsible for most of the problems presently facing the company. Between belches he dictates a memo to all executives soliciting suggestions on how to improve communications with company associates.

Mission of your memo:

- Be the first to get favorable attention. Drop what you are doing, even an "Operation Mother Lode," and get busy impressing Exalted One with your brilliance.
- Express strong agreement with his thesis that communications with associates stink and can be improved.
- You know how to use buzz words brilliantly and make fuzzy wording appear knowledgeable and thoughtful, and are, therefore, an expert in communications.
- Recommend a solution which makes you a hero but frees you from responsibility for results.
- Prompt Number One to regard you as top executive timber.

Your memo:

Mr. U. R. Hotstuff:

Communications with <u>all associates</u> are extremely important. They supply the major basis for their perception of management. In turn, their perception largely determines their work performance, i.e., favorable perception, good performance; unfavorable perception, bad performance. I agree that our communications do need improvement. The following strategic plan is presented as a means of solving this critical problem.

Uncovering the real problem. Feedback from associates on this subject would be faulty because they would tell us what they think we want to hear. An outside consulting firm with demonstrated expertise in the communications field can provide an information bank from which management can make withdrawals in constructing a communications system likely to accomplish long-term objectives.

Solving the problem. To maintain complete objectivity, select someone not presently associated with communications to choose the consulting firm best qualified on a cost/benefit basis to develop an action plan for improving communications. The implementation process should take the form of gradual, albeit steady, movement of activation as contrasted to the orbiting approach. [Don't laugh. Remember, you're impressing, not informing.] Proper prioritizing will, therefore, be the first undertaking.

Anticipated futurities. Engaging consultants may first appear to create substantial additional expense. But effective implementation of the action plan will produce a return (measurable) in the form of improved morale and its concomitant, increased production.

So great are the possibilities associated with this challenge that I hope I can make some contribution to the genesis and implementation of the plan.

I. M. EAGER
[Sign I with a flourish in green ink]

Unfortunately, not all memos are geared to keeping the help in line, outsmarting a rival, or impressing a superior. Sometimes you will be asked to explain why you screwed up.

Whenever you are placed on the defensive, try your best

to give a verbal explanation so you can use your speaking prowess and savoir faire to persuade the inquisitor you are truly as pure as the driven snow. If you are caught misstating or even misleading in your oral presentation, you can always talk your way out of the problem by claiming your listener misunderstood. Not so with a memo. Quid scripti, scripti! When you must write the excuse, be persuasive but damn careful with your facts.

Situation: Your boss, after reviewing the results of your "profit center" (the "in" term for each division), asks for a memo explaining why your earnings are down 52% and your expenses up 72%.

Mission of your memo:

- To bring your boss's blood pressure down, so reply immediately.
- Convince him you have everything under control and that what he now regards as a catastrophe is merely a temporary situation.
- Subtly pass the blame to others—"stupid competitors," poor marketing research, etc.
- Remind him, tactfully of course, that one must spend money to make money.
- The long-range outlook for your operation is very bright, even brilliant. (So don't even think of cutting my bonus this year!)

Your memo:

Mr. U. R. Tough:

Your memo requesting reasons for our operating results not being up to speed arrived when I had almost completed an analysis of results to date. That's why I am able to respond immediately.

I was extremely disappointed with the totals, but not surprised. As the year began to unfold it became clear to me demand was softening considerably more than the market research people had predicted. Most of our competitors didn't just react—they panicked by offering ridiculous deals and incentives. It quickly became a situation of matching their deals or their beating our pants off. <u>Neither you nor I are about to be beaten by these pantywaists</u>.

Resulting additional expenses did depress earnings for the first six months. <u>BUT</u> they maintained our market share and kept our products in a prominent place on the dealers' shelves. I confidently expect the payoff to start coming in during the second half, and really to boom next year.

Accordingly, we have revised our strategic plan to reflect realities of the market place, not predictions of what it will be. Our approach is bare knuckles—cut costs and sell benefits, not price, to produce a large quantity of <u>profitable business</u>. Unless the bottom falls out of the economy [always leave a loophole to crawl out of], you'll be seeing much better numbers at year's end and truly terrific ones next year.

I. M. Squirming
[Sign I with a flourish in green ink]

GENERAL GUIDELINES IN PREPARING A MEMO

Be careful when you plagiarize. It's OK to borrow ideas, phrases, and paragraphs from others—just don't get caught doing it. Lift material readers are unlikely to have seen in original form. Use the public library as the prime source for filched gems. Rare indeed is the subject not covered in a text available there. Most libraries have copiers, eliminating the drudgery formerly associated with plagiarizing.

Keep your buzz words up to date. Remember that buzz words and phrases have a life span, some longer than others. What for many years were subcontractors suddenly became "outsources"; goal has been replaced by "target." Search diligently for new buzz words and phrases and prune the ones which have been cast upon the discard pile. Avoid common ones and be bold enough to use those a bit on the avant-garde side. For example, "The findings of the study show" translates to "The printout on that program is."

Some buzz words seem to grow stronger with frequency of use: *optimum, interface, feedback, viability, profile, posture, prioritizing, input* (when *input* comes, *output* can't be far behind), *access,* and *bottom line* are prime examples. *Network* (as a verb) is moving quickly to the top of the charts.

Skip heroics and humility. Two contradictory sets of circumstances exist in most companies. One is the myth, what the hotshots think is happening; the other is the reality, what is *really* happening. In your memos focus on the myth and forget reality. Tell management what it wants to hear. Higher-ups seldom keep memos which disconcert them. To have one of your memos returned with a notation scribbled on the front rather than replied to by memo is to know that you have messed with the myth.

Even if company morale is at rock bottom never say so in a memo unless Exalted One thinks so, too. Forget what the other leading lights think. Remember that it is not in the nature of kings to question the loyalty of their subjects, only their worthiness.

Suppose your boss has asked for your ideas on an activity for which he has overall responsibility but which is directly managed by one of your peers. Keep your recommendations free of disclaimers of expertise. Never hedge with expressions of fraternal respect such as: "My proposals do not in any way imply that John's performance has been less than it should have been." Tough luck, John. The boss asked you to give him your ideas, and you're giving them. If the boss decides to put John's operation under you, so be it.

Make your memos memorable—for the right reasons. Each memo makes an impression—good, bad, or indifferent. Keep in mind that the latter two likely will be injurious, perhaps even fatal, to your career. Before sending a memo, check to make sure that all words are spelled correctly and used properly and that your grammar is at least acceptable.

Rewrite each memo at least once, sprinkling it with stardust to make it sparkle. Don't be afraid to use periods. Leave long, intricate sentences to highly skilled novelists. Avoid being too wordy, for long, multi-paged memos are sure turn-offs.

Never allow your secretary to send one of your memos before you have read it. "That was my secretary's fault" is unacceptable. Your name (and first initial in green ink) appears beneath the message.

"Outstanding memo writer" is one of the highest encomiums a role player can receive, but there is a potential pitfall here. You can become so proficient you end up writing memos for the top executives. That end is really a dead one.

CHAPTER 13

MAKE THE MOST OF EVERY MEETING

Few, very few, meetings serve a legitimate business purpose. But meetings offer ideal forums for role players to exhibit their talents. Here you are judged solely on what you say and how you say it. Act accordingly.

Plan your act carefully. Get a good seat. Some meetings are so stereotyped and humdrum that everyone always sits in the same place. If you are in such a tradition-bound company, follow protocol. If seats are not assigned, apply some imagination. Sit in a different seat each time. Avoid sitting next to or across from the leading light at the meeting. Try to position yourself as closely as possible to the end of the table, but first make sure you are not usurping the private property of a higher-up. The end of the table is most desirable because you can be seen without a lot of neck-straining and can maintain eye contact with all in attendance.

Sit straight, but be sure you appear relaxed. Exude confidence, as the tigers in the room feast on the diffident. Affix a slight smile. Do not lean back in the chair, as it is not only unseemly but also quite dangerous. One slip and back you go, designating you forever as an oaf.

Pay particular attention to your hands. Keep them folded on the edge of the table to signify confidence and control, both of which are prime executive qualities. Folding your arms is quite acceptable, but if continued for a prolonged period will wrinkle your sleeves. Chin cupped in hand contemplatively is also effective but should be done sparingly for maximum impact.

Watch your mannerisms. Avoid nervous manifestations such as squirming, yawning, twiddling your thumbs, or playing with a ring. Such actions indicate deep insecurities. Fondling a double chin, or even worse, a triple one, is not only gauche in the extreme, but also focuses attention on your lack of self-discipline which produced the layers of fat. Mentioning the prohibition against nail biting is unnecessary. Obviously insecure people such as nail biters are not invited to meetings. Do not look at your watch frequently. This habit indicates that you are overburdened, harassed, or, heaven forbid, bored.

Meetings are serious business—no loud laughter please. Executives are expected to be decorous at all times, never flippant. When the ranking executive at a meeting cracks a funny (as used here, funny is a comment he makes and at which he is the first to laugh), laughter is not only permitted, but required. Belly laughs or those of the knee-slapping variety are frowned upon even in responding to tales told by Peerless Leader.

Pick the right props. If the meeting is supposed to follow an agenda prepared and distributed in advance, bring a neat file folder for each discussion topic. On the front of each folder place a sticker showing the particular subject to which it relates. The file on top (to be seen by all) should be the one for the subject currently being discussed. Derive maximum effect from the folders by referring to them frequently. If you are actually reading the baseball scores, that is your business. As each subject is talked out, put the folder for that topic on the bottom of the pile.

Make sure that each folder contains at least two pieces of paper. Articles clipped from external sources such as newspapers and magazines are more impressive than internal memos or publications. Pertinent passages should be highlighted with a yellow marker to show that you have done your homework. It is preferable that the material in each folder be useful in your discussion, but any material, regardless of relevance, is better than none.

Whenever you refer to a file, do it without fumbling through piles of paper to find what you want. Top executives will not appreciate having to hold up proceedings while you fumble. More important, you will have destroyed the image of good organization the folders are supposed to create.

Keep a tablet, not just a note pad, in front of you throughout the meeting. Legal size is more impressive than 8½-by-11, and yellow more attention-getting than white. Always center the tablet in front of you to indicate a middle-of-the-road position, rather than leanings to either the left or right.

Tablets encased in leatherette covers create more favorable attention than do naked ones. A cover, providing it doesn't shriek "plastic," conveys a touch of class. Genuine leather will probably be regarded as a bit too much. If the cover bears an impressive logo showing it is a memento of a meeting you attended at a fancy resort or hotel, keep the folder closed except when taking notes. If you receive a cover to commemorate your attending a meeting at a Holiday Inn in Scranton, Pennsylvania, burn it immediately upon returning home, or even better, leave it in your room. It is OK to have your name imprinted on the cover in modest type. Gold is best, silver satisfactory, but white too garish. Covers bearing imprints of suppliers should not be displayed, lest you be suspected of being on the take. If a gift cover does not bear an imprint, use it. Take notes with a dignified, but not too fancy, automatic pencil. An ink pen, even the ballpoint variety, can be a bit messy.

To smoke or not to smoke cigarettes is a decision you should make before each meeting, even if you are a chain smoker. More and more higher-ups, especially those who have kicked the habit, openly express doubts about the smarts of anyone using anything proven to be harmful to health. When a higher-up of that bent of mind is present, don't smoke. Better to risk suffering a nicotine fit. Pipes remain acceptable with most people and are an ideal prop for affecting the phlegmatic pose. Cigars are allowed only if the one in charge of the meeting is a cigar smoker. Twirling eye glasses as you listen is a good act, but don't drop them.

Never use a tape recorder or dictating machine at a meeting. It is very stupid to demonstrate publicly that you either are too lazy to write or are such an egocentric that you defy any convention.

Win friends in high places and put down foes. Be artful in your note taking. Maintain maximum eye contact with the one you are making notes on. Rapt attention to what a superior is saying shows you are truly awed by the words spewing out. Eyeballing a rival serves notice that you will be checking the accuracy of what is being said. Your staring may even cause a bad presentation.

Write neatly so that anyone who glances at your notes will be impressed. And you can be sure that glances will be cast. Never record your honest opinion on what is said. A B S! noted in the margin can come back to haunt you.

Closely monitor the hotshots to make certain you take notes on what they consider important. Usually a facial expression or a vocal inflection conveying "OK, girls and boys, here it comes straight from Mount Sinai," is your cue to get your pencil moving on the paper. Delay long enough to nod your head several times, affix a look of enthrallment on your face, then write vigorously.

When a rival is pontificating, use more than eye contact to disrupt the flow. As word after word rolls off smooth tongue without stammer or pause, lay your pencil down and stare directly at poise personified. Have a quizzical look on your face which conveys: "Just what in the hell are you trying to say." The next time your eyes meet, shake your head from side to side to demonstrate your complete incredulity.

As hotshot's confidence begins to wane and poise starts to fade, move in for the kill. Pick up your pencil to be prepared to write furiously whenever rival makes a statement or answers a question. Use lots of underlines and exclamation points.

When a subordinate makes a bid for special attention by hamming it up in the presence of your superior, use your pencil and facial expressions to shoot down the underling. Glower throughout the performance, varying your looks from disgust to amazement. Write slowly and determinedly so that even the culprit knows you have written: "This son of a bitch and I are going to have a talk."

Attract favorable attention. When making a presentation at a meeting, understand that the eyes of those who count are on you. Speak effectively and affect impressive mannerisms as described in previous chapters.

Don't shout. Shouters are universally regarded as boors. Keep your voice level at a conversational tone. Don't preach or orate. Avoid nervous laughs.

Check crutch words and phrases at the door. "You know" should never pass your lips. If they know, why tell them. Also taboo are "I mean," "OK?," and "Isn't that right?" Insecures seek approval. True executives command it.

Give chalk talks as frequently as possible. A piece of plain, white chalk and a blackboard are the two most powerful tools available to a role player at a meeting. Use them. If your meeting room doesn't have a blackboard, utilize your persuasive powers to sell the higher-ups on installing one. In the meantime, buy a portable blackboard and put it on a tripod.

Always put your presentation on the blackboard before the meeting begins. Never bore leading lights by making them watch you write. Cover the board and unveil it just before you start talking. Drama is inherent in the unveiling process. Add more flair by unveiling in stages, uncovering each part just prior to discussing it.

List separately key ideas and phrases to give your audience a visual summary of what you said. Underlining major points also makes a good impression.

Many are the ways to gain attention and earn accolades from a chalk talk. None is more effective than the time-honored acrostic. Suppose you are outlining ways to stop a sales decline your company is experiencing. Summarize the major points of your plan so that at the end you have written:

see more customers every day
ask for orders on each call
leave out details, concentrate on benefits
eliminate errors
stay in touch with all customers

Heads of the bigwigs will begin to nod in approval of your ingenuity. Keep on going while you're hot. Return to the board. Now capitalize and underline the first letter of each thought so that you now have:

See more customers every day
Ask for orders on each call
Leave out details, concentrate on benefits
Eliminate errors
Stay in touch with all customers

The longer the hotshots look at the product of your genius, the more their eyes bug, the faster their hearts beat. Feel quite pleased if the Ranking One says, "By God, these are the steps we gotta take to get the sales curve going up again. Send a copy to everyone in the organization."

That you have broken no new ground or that all of these ideas are found in the first two chapters of basic sales courses is not important. What matters is that you have offered a simple solution, conveyed your ideas in an interesting way, and spared rulers of the roost the dreaded ordeal of making a tough decision.

All in the room, including CEO if he is present, associate your standing before a blackboard, chalk in hand, with the power figures of their pasts—teachers, coaches, and professors. Implicit in writing on a blackboard is leadership which deserves to be followed.

Keep up to date with the latest technological developments, too. Slides are fine if professionally done and the machine works. Overhead projectors can be impressive if you write on the acetate sheets with flair. Video tape is coming on strong, and more and more companies are adding video departments.

A meeting is also an arena for mental jousting. When it becomes apparent you are attracting favorable attention from the moguls, expect your rivals to use their devious minds and razor sharp tongues to cut you down. After you have determined which of your rivals are attracting favorable attention, use your own devious mind and razor-sharp tongue to make them meteors.

Enter each meeting prepared to wound your rivals and ward off their attacks. Welcome the combat, for mental jousting must be the favorite spot of anyone seeking to become king or queen. Here are typical situations encountered in meetings, and your appropriate course of action in each.

ON OFFENSE

Eager Beaver is spewing hyperbole about a new product, calling it the perfect item for tomorrow's marketplace.

Make eye contact with Eager, firmly but not hostilely, and ask: "What about the day after tomorrow? It always arrives sooner than expected. Remember what happened to CB radios? The companies that once flew high with them were shot down, zapped." Now who is the futurist in the room? Certainly not Eager.

Your biggest rival has just finished one hell of an effective presentation. Big boss's face glows with a "that's my shining light" smile. You will be tempted to cut. Resist temptation. Affect a smile as big as Number One's. On your way out, smile warmly at rival and to yourself say: "You son of a bitch, I'll get you next time." Then do it.

Gertie Gotfacts has the floor at the annual "staff retreat" held at a fancy resort in the hinterlands. She's responding to CEO's question: "Why, when the economy is surging, are both our sales and earnings declining?" "I have been wondering the same thing," Gertie says, "and consequently on my own have studied the situation thoroughly. My findings are that our competitive position has deteriorated severely in the past several years because our products are inferior, our service below average, and our dealer-support inadequate."

Gertie is right. But the look of disbelief on leader's face indicates he doesn't agree. Therefore Gertie is wrong.

You, and everyone in the room, know that product development, pricing, and service practices are rooted in the Ice Age. It's true that the company isn't growing. But what the hell, the executive class is living quite well without working up a sweat. What Gertie is talking about could lead to that most evil of business practices—cost cutting. Why start something that might rock the boat and maybe throw some people overboard?

As soon as Gertie finishes, say with a straight face: "You mentioned your study but didn't give us the findings of your marketing research. What does it show?"

All present do their best to stifle a hearty laugh. Marketing research? Who's kidding whom? Who around this place knows what marketing research is, let alone does any? But the others play your game. They are as opposed to boat-rocking as you are, and they also like the good life.

Don't give Gertie the opportunity to set you straight on what marketing research is and exactly what is involved in conducting a statistically sound program. Address your remarks to Gertie but say what Number One wants to hear. "Gertie, business today is very similar to how Hemingway described a bull fight: 'There is only one beast in the bull ring, the crowd.' The beast we are fighting is the customer, not the competition. We have an absolute need to know what our customers think and how they are most likely to act if we are to clip their horns rather than be gored by them. Conducting marketing research is the only viable means of basing our value judgments on solid facts rather than impressions."

You have given Exalted One a way out of his dilemma of facing a tough decision and he immediately takes it. "Marketing research, that's what we need. Let's get started right away." He may even put you in charge.

Don't worry about Gertie. Some "with it" company in the same industry is probably savvy enough to hire her.

ON DEFENSE

You have been asked for a progress report on a big deal project assigned to you. While you are talking, Harriet Hairsplitter interrupts to ask a question about a key aspect of the program, one you have completely overlooked. Without hesitating or losing a drop of poise, look her in the eyes and with a trace of disgust in your voice declare, "That's a detail. I am talking about the big picture." Put special emphasis on "big." As soon as the meeting is over, tie up the loose end before Harriet unravels your big deal.

You have been assigned the task of breathing new life into an annual sales campaign unchanged for so long that the only emotion it produces is ennui. You have developed some exciting new approaches that appeal to everyone except the diehard duo, Nay and Never. Nay speaks first: "I think you are establishing quite a few new precedents that will create many future problems." Never follows: "Many changes coming at the same time tend to confuse. Our people are accustomed to the present program. I say leave it alone." Nay adds quickly: "So do I."

Both Nay and Never reflexively resist change. They yearn for yesterday, for simpler times, when all golf balls were white. Had they spent as much time making positive contributions as they have worrying about people moving around them, fewer people would have moved around them. But one must credit Nay and Never with persisting in trying to cut down all comers. Now you are their target.

Do not brush off Nay and Never as mere curmudgeons frozen in the footsteps of yesterday, easily disposed of with one slash of the tongue. They are actually certified experts, through many years of practice, of attacking the ideas of others by raising all that could possibly happen if a new idea were adopted, rather than what would probably happen. Both know their future is their past, but by God, no one is going to move ahead of them without a fight.

Respond to Nay and Never by suggesting they function in an area in which they are totally incapable of performing—coming up with an alternate idea. "Understand, Nay and Never, that what is important here is the end, not the means. Joe (the boss) wants better results from the program. I'm sure that one look at sales figures for the past five campaigns explains why he is so dissatisfied." Say not another word until both of them give some sign of agreement with your premise, which they will have to do eventually, although quite reluctantly. "The plan I presented is one means of achieving our common end. If you have other ideas on how better to reach our goal of more sales, I'm sure Joe will be glad to have them in a memo. How soon will you need the memo, Joe?" "Tomorrow morning," bellows Joe. Nay and Never begin immediately to look for another comer to try to squelch.

You and your peers are making your monthly report to your boss on significant past happenings and upcoming developments in your respective areas. Tired Tirade, whose mission in life is to demonstrate his own brilliance and everyone else's stupidity, is at it again. After taking up most of the time allowed for the meeting with a fustian account of goings on in his operation to prove what a dynamic leader he is, Tired has shifted to phase two, demonstrating the stupidity of everyone else in the room. Tired consistently interrupts each speaker, frequently in mid-sentence, to question why something is being done the way it is. Tired is self-centered, but he is not stupid. He knows his tactics disconcert.

When Tired asks you his first question, pause ten or fifteen seconds, smile at him somewhat patronizingly, then respond: "Tired, I'm telling you what time it is. Apparently, you want to know how a watch works. Let me know when it is convenient for you to stay after hours and I will tell you all you want to know about this project." Move quickly to your next subject.

You are attending an out-of-town meeting of the company. Being invited to attend provides you a golden opportunity to strut your stuff in the grand manner and is, as the politicians say, a high honor and privilege. Probably relatively few in your peer group will be so honored. If this is your first out-of-town meeting, the natives are going to be very restless, wondering why in the hell you are going and they are not. Play it down. Call your attendance at the meeting merely part of your responsibilities, and declare that work is work wherever it has to be done. Make it clear that you certainly don't expect to have any fun at the Ultra Swank By The Sea Resort. Actually, you are going there neither to have fun nor to work. You are going there to make favorable impressions.

Spruce up your wardrobe a bit. Women should avoid the chic or daring. Men should avoid loud jackets or slacks. Be sure several sweaters and/or shirts include a polo pony or alligator (no substitutions, please). If you belong to a country club, wear something which includes the club's logo.

If you have not been assigned to work on advance meeting arrangements, somehow get yourself involved, even on such piddling assignments as directing the shipping of meeting supplies or arranging seating assignments at the banquets. Of course these duties are no big deal, but role players must excel at making big deals out of little deals.

Preparing for an out-of-town company meeting affords you an unusual opportunity to depict activity as if it were usefulness. Take full advantage of your unusual opportunity. Maintain a harried look on your face at all times.

Conduct a number of conferences to demonstrate to all reviewing your performance you are making damn sure that all assignments you have delegated to others are being carried out as you instructed. Keep asking those in charge of the meeting how you can help them.

Doing all of the above not only creates a favorable impression but can also earn you a pleasant perk—membership on the go early, stay late squad. Meeting planner, being a good salesman to have landed that cushy job, will probably have persuaded the boss that every meeting requires at least two days preparation on site and a similar amount of time for cleaning up after meeting details. Surely the planner can't be expected to handle all the many onerous tasks that must be done to start and wind up a meeting. These sybaritic days of gourmet food, barrels of booze, and fun in the sun will be ample reward for your extra efforts which earned you a place on the squad.

When CEO and the other hotshots arrive on meeting day, make sure you are much too involved in making big deals out of little deals to greet them upon their arrival. Mingle sparingly with the muckety-mucks during the meeting. This is a time for action, not talk, to be observed getting things done, not standing around visiting. If you perform effectively, the top executives will surely commend you for the outstanding job you did in helping make the meeting such a great success. Management always regards each out-of-town meeting as a great success, never as a mere success. Perhaps that is because meetings cost a great deal of money.

Make sure you handle all of your assignments flawlessly. If one of your betters is about to make a serious error of omission or commission, go to the rescue. When a peer is in the same situation, let the peer blow it.

It is very important that you favorably impress company associates from the boondocks who are attending the meeting, especially if they are sales types. Leading lights spend most of their time at a meeting assuring sales types of their vital importance to the company, so listen, at least act as if you are listening, to the opinions they express. Most sales types hold strong opinions on practically every subject and express them freely. If they think favorably of you, and tell the hotshots, you are a cinch to become a regular at such meetings.

To produce the desired result, buy lots of drinks for the attendees. Laugh at their raunchy jokes without blushing—ribald stories go with the territory. Go out of your way to add to their enjoyment of the meeting. Sales types are accustomed to fending for themselves, so they are especially grateful for acts of personal kindness.

Before leaving your room each morning follow these two practices: one, screw on a pleasant smile, making sure it looks sincere; two, check your inner tape player to be certain that "How nice to see you", "I have heard so many nice things about you that I have really looked forward to meeting you," "Isn't this a great meeting?," "How is your family?," and other inanities flow freely upon command. Both the screwed-on smile and robotical greetings are essential in appearing happy and friendly. Unhappy and unfriendly people are not regarded as assets at meetings. Constantly remind yourself of the need to bubble up.

Quite rare is the out-of-town meeting without at least one incident. Some incidents are relatively minor, while others keep the gossip mill grinding away for months.

If a delegate with a snootful of booze falls down the stairs and breaks a leg or arm, perhaps both, that's no big deal. Boys will be boys and girls will be girls. If someone loses a lot of money in a poker or crap game, that incident is classified as a small deal unless the spouse of the loser complains to higher-ups, in which case transgression advances to semi-big deal. If a man beats his wife, regardless of the stated reason, that is a big deal. If a wife beats her husband, that is his problem. Stealing a feel or pinching can be a small deal, semi-big deal, or big deal, depending upon the relative status of the feeler and feelee and pincher and pinchee. Making love to someone else's spouse is always a federal case. Alleging that the other party was the aggressor will not absolve the culprit from the severe penalty imposed for committing a sin of the flesh.

It is understood, of course, that you will not be involved personally in an incident. Not being a participant is not enough to exonerate you from all responsibility and attendant consequences. Any company must take prompt and proper action to punish anyone causing a big deal or federal case which casts a pall over the meeting. Sometimes, but not often, semi-big deals are judged to require adjudication to determine guilt and assess punishment.

In pursuit of swift and equitable justice, a high-level strategy meeting will be called immediately. If preliminary findings indicate that a probable federal case has occurred, CEO may serve as Chief Justice. Witnesses will be called. Statements will be taken. Questions will be asked and all answers carefully evaluated. Eyebrows will be raised. Chins will be stroked. The easiest way out will be sought.

If you were at or near the scene of such an incident, you will be a witness called, questioned, and evaluated, not a promising situation for anyone with executive-suite aspirations. Remember the ruin which befell one of the all-time great role players because of unrelenting efforts to learn what he knew and when he knew it.

To stay free of even the slightest tint of incident involvement, first avoid the places incidents are most likely to occur—barrooms and the bedrooms of others. All those indicating the slightest tendency to be incident-prone, such as heavy boozers and lover boys or girls, should be shunned. Stay far away from card or dice games. Keep your distance from quarreling couples.

Even after taking these and other precautions common sense tells you to take, should you become involved either directly or indirectly in an incident which is deemed by the powers-that-be to be a federal case or big deal, keep your cool. Don't volunteer that you were present at the scene of the crime unless eyewitnesses placed you there. If you are summoned to testify, play down your knowledge of the dastardly deed with a disclaimer, such as you were talking shop or taking care of a meeting assignment and were so engrossed in what you were doing that you were oblivious to what was going on around you. Regardless of the excuse you give, always insist you didn't see a thing.

Upon returning to the office, don't volunteer any information about the meeting. When asked, say it was a great meeting and add quickly that putting it on was work, damn hard work. Tell no tales about either the sinners or the saints.

Also exercise caution in discussing the meeting with your friends in the outside world. Never refer to the time spent on the beach, golf course, or tennis court. Word of your goofing off might trickle to some top executives in your company, which assures your being cut from future meeting arrangements squad.

You are presiding at a meeting of subordinates. Here you are the Big One. You don't have to impress anyone present, but all those present had damn well better impress you.

Each time you preside at a meeting of lessers, as you look around the table and smile to light the way for the benighted, always ask yourself two questions: "What can each of them do for me?"; "What can each of them do to me?" Act according to your answers. Reward friends and punish would-be rivals.

Support your followers to the fullest. As they talk, nod your head as a symbol of agreement. Affix a slight smile on your face to show your approval of their performance. As they finish, congratulate them on a good job. During a meeting, reward your friends with cushy assignments or announce they will be attending a seminar at a fancy resort to let all the troops know what it takes to get ahead in your outfit.

Show absolutely no mercy to all those demonstrating the ambition and ability to become a star. Stop them before they become genuine, honest-to-God rivals by practicing a method used by the Mennonites—shunning. Keep them out of as many meetings as you can. As one is talking, shake your head from side to side to signal your disagreement. Interrupt frequently to contradict. When one attempts humor, frown a bit.

Go public with your punishment of would-be rivals. Announce that one fallen from favor will now report directly to your assistant. Call it an "administrative streamlining measure." Don't give any indication the boom is being lowered. Allowing everyone to see the shock on the miscreant's face is the best way to eliminate the competitive spirit in other would-be usurpers of your power and perks.

Be especially on guard against potential rivals attempting to sabotage you when your boss is present. Expect them to try to upstage you. Just don't let them succeed. So as not to appear petty or paranoid to your boss, don't put down a rival as sharply as you would if your boss were not present. Remember, too, that in holding up hoops for your rivals to jump through, you may come off as a bit of a brute or perhaps somewhat stupid. If you ask an underling who is threatening your security to "clarify what you are trying to say" and your boss says he understands and asks "don't you?," you have damaged yourself, not the traitorous one.

Cut off would-be threats before they have an opportunity to demonstrate their talents to your boss. Outline to each the format to be followed. Shake up all of them with such specific commands as "There will be no histrionics to impress the chief, understand? Stick to the facts, then shut up."

Keep an especially sharp eye on anyone your boss has commented on favorably. If at all possible, exclude all of your subordinates in that category from a meeting at which the boss is present. If the boss asks you why so-and-so isn't there, tell him, "Oh, Mary is OK in her specialty, but she tends to get lost on an unfamiliar track." Specialists seldom make executives.

You are most vulnerable when your boss calls a meeting and asks you to bring an eager underling. You are doing your best to make the boss's favorite a goner, but you can't let the boss in on your secret. Worst of all, the no-good is smart, scheming, and shrewd.

Watch the boss all the time the scoundrel is talking. Check the boss's every reaction. When the boss begins to stare at you, look away momentarily but start watching again as soon as the coast is clear.

As soon as the unfaithful servant has completed his or her spiel, determine quickly if your boss considered the ideas to be great, good, fair, or ridiculous. In the unlikely event the grade is ridiculous, immediately express your scorn for your underling's presentation and your chagrin that any of your associates would be so far off base. If the grade appears to be fair, express mild disagreement with the big mouth. If it is good, search your brain for an idea you can add on in the hope that the final plan will become known as your idea. If, however, the boss's grade is great, start immediately on getting Benedict Arnold transferred to another department.

Never make a suggestion at a meeting attended by your boss if there is even a somewhat reasonable chance he or she prefers an idea proposed by someone else. The rule which applies here is that when you are not certain of winning, don't get into the game. Wait for better playing conditions.

Use meetings with subordinates to learn what is going on in other parts of the company, particularly those headed by major rivals. Try to uncover inferior performance, real or alleged, which can be cited as reasons, at least as excuses, for your operation's difficulties. Make sure all of your lessers understand that intelligence-gathering is not only encouraged, it is rewarded.

Employ subordinates as your spear carriers in in-house quarrels. Never sully your hands with such messes. Subtly encourage your lackeys to raise hell with how your peers are running their operations.

Always keep your troops guessing about how you are going to act at a meeting. Vary your moods to confuse them. Be all smiles at one, scowl throughout the next; praise lavishly at one, chew ass vigorously at another. Be liberal with your personal references. Use lots of "I think," "I know," and, of course, "I told the big boss."

Keep in mind that the major purpose of each convocation of your underlings is to instill in them the unfaltering conviction that you are a real comer. Make sure all understand that anyone who doesn't pay obeisance to you will soon be a goner.

CHAPTER 14

TRAVEL WITH ECLAT

Business people who do not travel do not go far. Business travel comes in three varieties: high status, low status, and no status. Try to begin traveling at the high-status level, but settle for low status if you must. If your travel is no status, give up role playing or find a new company.

High-status travel involves using airlines exclusively. Travel must be to large cities and swanky resort areas throughout the country to merit high status. Travel limited to a few cities, even glamorous ones, is not enough. Staying in well-known, prestigious hotels is another high-status requirement.

Low status is attached to flying to the same cities, renting a car to make calls in surrounding towns, staying in motels, and eating at local steak houses. Even many truck drivers vary their travels.

Covering a territory by car offers absolutely no status, not even if you drive a Mercedes. Granted, some low-status travelers, especially manufacturers' representatives, make a lot of money. But to a genuine role player, money is not a satisfactory substitute for status.

High-status travelers must talk a lot about their travels to derive maximum benefit from their wanderings. Nothing impresses those both inside and outside the company more than hearing about recent trips and upcoming ones.

Low-status travelers may talk about their flights but should be mute on hotels stayed in and restaurants frequented. Mentioning flight numbers demonstrates you are an experienced air traveler. No-status travelers should discuss their journeys only with their spouses, customers, and bankers.

Act like a seasoned traveler. Even on your first trip you must play the role of seasoned traveler. Observe the professional travelers in your company and adapt their techniques.

Using an obviously new suitcase on your first trip shouts "amateur traveler." Avoid embarrassment. Even if you have a new, leather one, don't take it to the airport in its pristine form. With a demonstration of will matching that of G. Gordon Liddy's, somehow call up the courage to give it a couple of scuffs and nicks. Checking a beat-up bag spares you the indignity of being patronized by the ticket agent as an unseasoned traveler. You need not be concerned after that, for when you pick it up at your destination it will probably look as if it belongs to a member of a million miles club.

Join one of the airlines' clubs to be able to display the baggage tag symbolic of such membership. In time you will want to display several such tags.

Carry a garment bag with name and logo of an airline. Never use one provided by a local haberdashery. Avoid any provided as advertising, even one of your own company's. Role players are dignified, never walking billboards.

Working on the plane is an absolute must. Once "the wheels are in the well," open your briefcase and get busy. Reading files or reports or using your calculator is OK, but writing reports on a yellow legal pad is much more impressive. The impression given is added to substantially by lay-ing your pencil down periodically to peer into the wild blue yonder to make it appear you are conceiving a thought.

When the booze lady or man pulls the cart full of temptation beside you, opt for soda or coffee if you are going to conduct any business the remainder of the day. If you are free of business involvement until the morrow, have one, perhaps even two if you are so inclined. One martini can be too much. That particular concoction has ruined many acts because of its almost sinister power to change the timid into fighters and wallflowers into passionate lovers.

Conversing with your seat mates is seldom productive and never impressive. Likely they are also role players, so chances are you will try to snow each other and end up in a stalemate. It is highly unlikely you will encounter a CEO on a commercial airliner. Practically all of them use their company jets. Anyway, Exalted Ones probably are in first class. You had better be in coach.

Although it is highly unlikely you will meet anyone on a plane worth trying to impress, it is probable you will sit next to people who act like Number Ones. Waste not your talents on them. Act as if you are totally engrossed in writing your reports. When one talks, keep your eyes on your tablet and occasionally say "pardon me." Eventually, he or she will get the message and shut up.

On occasion women will find themselves seated with charming, handsome men and men will be distracted by attractive women nearby. This is not a handbook on sexual conquest. Plenty of this variety are presently in print. Go ahead and play the role of big, important executive, but be very cautious about playing around, even to the extent of agreeing, or persuading seat mate to agree, to sharing a taxi into the city. There is always the possibility that someone who knows you will witness your attempt to play sex symbol and give your spouse or a top executive in your company an exaggerated account of your alleged transgression. If your purpose is indeed honorable—to save money—eat dinner in a deli. If your purpose is dishonorable, better think again.

Never return from a meeting with a suntan. The sun shines outside. Meetings are held inside. Ergo, suntans acquired at meetings reveal that pleasure did indeed triumph over business. Walking into the office in the midst of winter with a bronze tint to the face shouts to the pale faces, "I am a cheating, insufferable cad." It is also very stupid.

To satisfy both nontravelers in your firm and the Internal Revenue Service, a business trip must be total travail, completely free of any of life's little pleasures. So keep quiet about any of your activities not involving work, even if that means staying silent about the entire trip.

Don't be a sucker. Before traveling to a city for the first time, learn something about the town in advance—the best hotels and restaurants and the fanciest watering holes. Also determine clip joints to avoid. Find out the distance between the airport and your hotel, and the most direct route. Such foreknowledge should prevent your taxi driver from giving you a sightseeing tour of the city and your ending up with a fare which pops the eyes of your expense account checker. When in doubt, take the bus.

Until you are firmly established in your company as an effective on-the-roader, be very cautious about allowing clients to select the restaurant when you invite them to dinner. Be especially wary in larger cities. Most have well-known, prestigious restaurants which are very much the place to be seen. The only truly outstanding feature of many of these fancy places, though, is the big check the waiter brings. Customers love to wine and dine on fat expense accounts so they can go to places they can't afford on their own. Many clients have no compunction about taking advantage of your hospitality, rationalizing they are paying for the entertainment by doing business with your company, or even thinking about doing business with you.

Keep in mind at all times that the green eyeshade folks in the accounting department are looking for ways to trip you before you have firmly established yourself as a traveler. Reporting big expenses (unreasonable is the term applied by the numbers mechanics) before you are considered a seasoned traveler can quickly ground you.

Pick the place before you invite. Make sure you select a restaurant the natives consider a "nice place," offering good food at something approaching reasonable prices. Being too miserly can cost you that client's business, an outcome certain to displease the moguls.

Extending a client a spur-of-the-moment invitation to lunch can also be perilous. Avoid creating a situation which might allow a customer to announce to the entire staff, "Come on, we are all going to lunch on XYZ company." People seldom invited to lunch are likely to order three martinis and the biggest steak on the menu. More damaging than the size of the bills are the reasons for it. When you explain what happened to the expense account checkers, and an explanation will surely be requested, you will have to admit that the customer controlled you. Anyone who doesn't control every situation will soon be restricted to the office.

TALES OF YOUR TRAVELS

A trip can build status only if it is discussed extensively. When reviewing your trip with others in your company, make it sound like a brain-draining, bone-tiring, and close-to-excruciating, but nevertheless "productive" experience. Be careful not to overdo your lamentations. Some higher-up may judge you psychologically unfit for travel and order you locked to your desk in perpetuity. If this fate befalls you, you will quickly learn what Thomas Gray really meant when he wrote "Full many a flower was born to blush unseen, and waste its sweetness on the desert air."

Talking to people outside your office about the exciting things you did and the swanky places you visited on a trip is not only permissible, it is, in fact, absolutely necessary. Why travel if you can't impress someone?

Use a Janus-like approach when discussing your trips: to your associates in the company display the face of unstinting devotion to the completion of your appointed rounds, of self-sacrifice in always placing company above self in performing tasks; to your friends in the outside world affect the face of unmistakable urbanity, and describe the plush places visited, the swanky restaurants patronized, the prominent people met, and the pleasures of life enjoyed. Just be certain to show the right face to the right audience.

Situation: You have just returned from a week in Hawaii. You are asked: "How was your trip?"

Face of devotion and self-sacrifice: "In a word . . . exhausting. Some people lay over for a night on the West Coast to soften the jet lag from the six-hour time change. My tight schedule forces me to take the whole chunk in one bite. When you arrive it is midnight at home but only six o'clock in the evening there. When your internal alarm clock awakens you at seven A.M. it is only one A.M. there. So you toss and turn until three or four, then finally get out of bed, totally beat. You work like fury, then have to socialize with clients to get the signature on the order form. Got home Sunday and even though I was bushed I spent the evening putting together what I accomplished."

Face of unmistakable urbanity: "The islands are heavenly. Just love the beautiful beaches. But I left my bikini in the room . . . had to cover myself like a nun so I wouldn't come back looking like a native. Frank, the kids, and the people at the office would accuse me of doing nothing but sunning and funning. I visited all the islands. That's called "client development" on the expense report. Arranged a Japanese Tea House party for my best clients. We had a ball. The shops are fascinating—expensive but fascinating. Almost needed a trunk for the stuff I bought.

Situation: It is January 15. The temperature at 2 P.M. is six degrees above zero. Twelve inches of snow are on the ground. A blizzard, on the wings of a thirty miles per hour wind, is in progress. Last week you were in Los Angeles. Next week you will be in Miami. You are asked: "How in the hell do you manage to finagle trips to warm places at this time of the year?"

Face of devotion and self-sacrifice: "Finagle your ass. I made forty-eight calls and three speeches last week. In Miami I am making a series of presentations on which I am working night and day because they can mean one hell of a lot of business for this company. So what if it does turn out to be warm? I'll be too busy to leave the hotel. Traveling on business may sound glamorous, but the only thing it is really good for is the ulcer medicine business."

Face of unmistakable urbanity: "Good planning, my friend, good planning. Switched from the Beverly Hills where I usually stay to the Century Plaza. Lots of action there. You should see the would-be starlets around that place. Showing off their wares to the movie moguls who hang out there, I guess. Some wares! Played the L.A. Country Club, probably the most exclusive in the country, maybe in the world. Went to Palm Springs to play a round at Thunderbird. I have played 83 of the top 100 courses as ranked by a golf magazine. Alice likes Miami a hell of a lot more than I do. I'm just doing one presentation a day. The whole deal, with questions, takes less than an hour. Probably not much business will come out of it, but a least it gets Alice out of the snow and off my back. I'll have plenty of time to run up to Boca Raton and loosen up my swing."

Create opportunities for travel. As you proclaim the agonies of travel to other office associates, always create opportunities for more high-status travel. Attend every seminar you can which bears the slightest relationship to your type of business or your particular responsibility. You won't experience difficulty in finding a large number of them. Every working day at least a dozen seminars of some type are being held on every business subject, real or imagined. Be selective in choosing which ones to attend. Base your decision on the people conducting the sessions, the after-hours events included in the registration fee, and the city and hotel in which it is to be held.

Seminars conducted by nationally known celebrities or those which include a well-known speaker or two are most desirable, for they add an important dimension to your name dropping act: "As Senator So-and-So said in a conversation with an intimate group at a seminar I attended recently," or "As Frank Famous told me at a reception at a meeting."

Look for sessions conducted at a leisurely pace, spread over three to five days, with the desired mix of business and pleasure. Give first preference to those with afternoons free for "individual discussions and idea exchanges." That the individual conferences will take place at the pool, on the golf course, or at the tennis courts is no one else's business. Skip all seminars held at airport hotels unless you want all work and no fun . . . and no bragging rights.

As to location, any island in Hawaii is by far number one in providing the desired combination of prestige and enjoyment twelve months of the year. San Francisco is second. Well-known resort hotels in season are always good. Phoenix, and Palm Springs are delightful in late autumn, winter, and early spring, but are hot houses in summer months. San Diego is good year around, but Los Angeles is congested and smoggy. Off-season rates save your company money, but offer you absolutely no status. Put prestige potential and your personal comfort index before savings to your firm.

New England resorts are ideal in summer and early autumn. Those in the Catskills and Poconos are pretty good, too. Colorado, especially Vail and Aspen, are now prestigious summer sites as well as skiing attractions.

Las Vegas is still an in spot, but Atlantic City seems to be gaining on it. Be very careful in either place. You can get in lots of trouble at the gaming tables.

New York City, referred to by seasoned travelers as the "Big Apple" or "Big A," is a must. To be forced to admit to never having been to the "Big Apple" is to your standing as a traveler what being the child of a coal miner is to your position in the social register.

Your written report detailing the new smarts you picked up at the seminar must be impressive enough to justify the large expenses incurred on your trip. Begin working on the memo immediately upon returning to the office or, even better, on the plane trip home. "So valuable were the ideas presented that I am writing this memorandum of significant ideas obtained on the flight home" is an opening line of which any role player can be proud.

Although protocol requires that the memo be addressed to your immediate boss, your goal should be to make it so impressive that ultimately it will end up before the eyes of Number One, or at least a leading light. Make it so scintillating that it will become the standard for memos on seminars by which others are judged.

Any seminar worthy of the name distributes workbooks

or summaries of all the topics covered. Some even provide a complete transcript of what was said. Under no circumstances allow anyone in the company to see this material. Some heroic cost-cutter will surely recommend buying the material instead of permitting executives to attend the seminars.

An important by-product of attending seminars is the contacts made with other attendees. Cultivate, and keep in touch with, those presently holding important positions and ones displaying obvious top executive potential.

Belong to and be active in trade groups covering your specialty. Most of them hold meetings at least once a year at a fancy hotel or resort. Few allow work to interfere with fun.

Women should not join a business association whose membership is limited to women. You seek to be regarded by the hotshots as a business *executive,* not as a business *woman.* That's a distinction with a decided difference.

At the first meeting you attend, carefully analyze the political dynamics of the association to determine who the kingmakers are. Once you have spotted them, curry their favor and volunteer for assignments which will put you in close contact with power. Serving on association committees can advance your political career and create another source of trips. Seek appointment to the committee which holds the most meetings during the year. Being chair of a committee is a must. Your goal is to start "through the chairs," eventually becoming president. This high honor will not only add to your prestige in the company, but will also provide you lots of nice trips and desirable perks throughout the year of your reign. Your preeminence in your field should also make you more attractive to other companies.

TRAVELS WITH CEO

Someday your phone will ring and the person on the other end of the line will invite you to take a business trip with Peerless Leader. The caller won't be Number One, but rather a secretary or a secretary's secretary. This moment of extraordinary exhilaration comes to every truly rising executive. If, after two or three years of playing executive you haven't received such a call, recognize that you aren't going anywhere in that company.

Nonchalance of a high degree is called for in such situations. Your tone of voice must be steady and calm, without the slightest trace of nervousness. Don't accept the invitation immediately. Instead answer "Just a minute while I check my schedule to see if I am open on those dates." Of course, if you have a conflict, you are going to get unconflicted fast. But you have carried out your charade of acting as if you regard your journey with Number One as just another business trip.

All arrangements for the trip will be made by CEO's secretary. Manage the situation so that your secretary deals with those from on high to impress them with your executive skills.

Traveling with Exalted One is one area of business still limited almost entirely to men, other than female secretaries. Perhaps this restriction results from leader's being more comfortable with the "club atmosphere" male associates provide. And, of course, some have not yet accepted the fact that women can perform as executives. Mrs. CEO also may be a factor.

Women may, however, be included in a group traveling with the big boss. A woman traveling in the entourage will likely be treated with great deference throughout the trip and probably not assigned any menial tasks. Being on the road with CEO, even in a group, offers a woman role player an excellent opportunity to display her skills to Number One. Demonstrate you can perform as well as the boys without trying to be one of them.

Any woman invited to solo with Exalted One is well advised to check his track record with women in the company and to determine exactly what kind of business he has in mind. Make sure your role isn't mistress to the master.

Outward bound. If your show owns a corporate jet, chances are excellent that you will be on it when you travel with CEO. When you arrive at the airport, greet him cordially but don't attempt to start a conversation. It is his prerogative to begin a conversation with whom he wants to talk and on the subject he wants to talk about.

Allow Mighty One to board first, not merely as a symbol of his position, but also to eliminate all possibility of committing the grievous sin of sitting in "his seat." Don't sit next to him, or if the configuration has facing seats, across from him. Your gambit here is to appear calm and confident. The farther you are away from him on the plane, the easier it will be for you to be calm and confident.

If you take off before nine A.M., bring a copy of the *Wall Street Journal* and start reading it shortly after the wheels are up. If you depart after nine A.M., read *Fortune, Business Week,* or even *Forbes.* Every executive is expected to start the business day with the WSJ, and that means long before nine A.M.

Before going into your next act, check his mood. If he wants to talk, listen a lot and talk very little. If he is silent, you be silent. Pull out your yellow tablet and write a report, at least give the appearance that you are. If he asks if anyone wants coffee, go immediately to the plane's serving station and begin taking coffee orders. It is understood that the steward's duties are always performed by the lower ranks on board. Don't wait to be told. Demonstrate that you know how the system works and are prepared to conform to it. Don't spill any coffee. Play it safe. Pour the cups half full.

If you leave in the afternoon or evening, CEO, ever the genial host, will likely ask if anyone wants a drink. He may even say, "Will you join me in a drink?" Decline his offer with profuse thanks. You are tense. Remember, too, that high altitude reduces tolerance for alcohol. Don't debut with loose tongue or slurred speech. Serve the others all the booze they want but limit yourself to coffee or soft drinks.

He may ask if you are interested in playing a game of gin rummy for modest stakes. If you are a better than average gin player, take him up on his offer. Allow him to win, but not by much. Your winning big is sure to bring an icy stare, followed by: "You must play a lot of gin to be so good. How do you find time to work? Ha! Ha! Ha!" Some captains of industry excel at conveying actual thoughts through apparent jest. If you don't play well, beg off by claiming you have to finish your important report. To play badly is to demonstrate that you are not very smart.

Expect CEO to subject you to rigorous cross-examination sometime during the trip to determine for himself if you are a legitimate comer. Be prepared to play "Information Please" at any time. Very likely he has reviewed your official company biography and your performance evaluations to date. Be sure your answers agree with the information in your biography.

His approach will be decidedly avuncular, the conversation quite low key. Do not be beguiled. Recognize his true purpose and answer accordingly. Questions will cover such areas as:

- family background
- education
- previous experience
- social standing
- hobbies

You will learn eventually if you passed or failed his quiz by whether or not you are again included in his entourage.

How you conduct yourself upon arrival at your destination will vary according to the purpose of your trip. But clearly understand that regardless of why you are there, the leader calls all the shots.

A meeting of your industry's trade association. That you were asked to join CEO at a meeting so near and dear to his heart offers positive evidence that someone up there in the executive suite does indeed like you. At such meetings, he rubs shoulders and trades war stories with his peer group. If he is a past or present officer of the association, or a member of the elite power group which determines the industry's position on important issues and decides who will express them, he will be regarded as a genuine celebrity and bowed and scraped to accordingly. Whether he is a power broker or just another member of the association, you can be certain he will display to his peers in the association only those from his company who are regarded as rising stars.

Your role here is strictly that of aide-de-camp which requires your being available to him twenty-four hours a day. But it is not necessary for you to walk one pace to his left and one pace behind him.

Don't be surprised if Big Boss skips all or most of the business meetings. Some CEOs much prefer to work the hallways and chat informally with their equals or attend a high-level strategy conference in someone's fancy suite.

You are to attend all meetings from gavel to gavel. If several sessions covering different subjects are held at the same time, attend parts of each and obtain copies of all material distributed. That night in your room read all the material so you can answer any questions CEO might ask about the sessions.

If you took your pride with you, keep it in the hotel check room throughout your stay. In performing your role of aide-de-camp, you are going to be executing a number of nonexecutive duties, some of which may be downright demeaning. To accept your role without resentment, apply one of the oldest and most frequently quoted clichés in business: "Anyone seeking to succeed must be willing to pay the price of success."

Should Number One deign to attend a business session, don't sit next to him unless he specifically requests the pleasure of your company. But keep an eye on him so you can be available immediately when he beckons for service.

Introduce yourself to a large number of meeting attendees. Don't limit your mingling to the other aides-de-camp present. Introduce yourself to and visit with some higher-ups. Try to obtain some inside information on each CEO or high executive you meet to determine the powerful ones worth impressing.

Always be seen talking to someone before a session or during a break. If and when Great One attends a business session you can be sure that he will observe personally how you are fitting into the group, known officially as your interpersonal relationship score. Observing you may be his only reason for attending a meeting. Your goal should be to be graded "one who relates to others easily and effectively."

Make such a strong, favorable impact on the leading players from other companies that you meet that they tell your leader how impressive you are. Should he not receive any favorable comments on your performance, he will probably wonder what you were doing to end up such a nonentity.

A meeting of your company's people in the hinterlands. At such a meeting, you must blend into the background. The folks who carry the firm's banner in the boondocks, far from the comfort and security of the Mother House, have come to see, hear, talk to, and touch the cloak of their hero—the CEO of their company.

Chances are excellent he will give a pep talk to the troops, for rare as the American bald eagle is the CEO who doesn't delight in performing before friendly, enthusiastic audiences. Your main responsibility is to see that his act comes off snag-free. Don't blow it!

If he is using slides, do not be so stupid as to get stuck running the projector. Too many things can happen to that damn machine, all of which are bad. Arrange for a local audiovisual expert to run the projector. Make it abundantly clear to this expert when you hire him or her that payment will be made only if the presentation is goof-free.

Also beware of being assigned to putting the master's voice on tape for posterity. Get an expert to do it so you don't end up with a tape emitting only humming noises.

If CEO uses flips charts in his presentation, reconcile yourself to the inevitable—you will flip the charts. Admittedly, making your debut before the folks in the precincts as a chart flipper is not exactly an auspicious beginning. Swallow your pride and concentrate only on flipping the right chart at the right time. Avoid all eye contact with the audience as you flip boring chart after boring chart, so you won't be discomfited by amused expressions on the faces of the audience. They don't intend to be derisive, but even you'll admit that it does look funnier than hell to see a nattily attired, properly coiffured, and obviously suave business executive flipping charts.

Fill the time not taken by business meetings to become personally acquainted with as many locals as you can. It is vital that you impress them enough that they tell CEO how able you are and how fortunate the company is to have someone of your high caliber on board.

Exercise great caution at the cocktail parties. Go easy on the booze to prevent your tongue's becoming loosened and your libido supercharged.

A public relations visit to a city important to the company. The size of the public reception accorded CEO will be proportionate to your firm's impact on the town, or on his national reputation. Even if neither your company nor its leader has enough clout to bring the media out for interviews or Chamber of Commerce types swarming to a luncheon to honor Great One, you can be sure that the Local Mogul who arranged the visit is on top of the world. Local will meet the plane and whisk his hero and you away to keep the busy schedule.

If you haven't met your host before, keep in mind that Local, being carried away with the thought of leader's pilgrimage, will not remember your name. So give Local your business card to save both of you embarrassment.

If CEO is interviewed by the media, limit your role to that of interested observer. Answer no questions, make no statements, do not allow yourself to be included in any photos. Don't even give your name to reporters. The presence of Peerless Leader in town is the story, and don't you get in the way of it.

At a luncheon arranged by Local for good customers and the town's bigwigs, sit where you are told. Converse with your table neighbors, focusing on them, their business, and their opinions, rather than on you and your importance. It is unlikely they will be so overwhelmed by your performance they will take the time to express their admiration of you to CEO. But they may mention you favorably to Local who might pass on the good words about you. Every favorable comment moves you a mite closer to the top.

CEOs are quite fond of talking about their companies to anyone who will listen, but especially so to two particular audiences: big customers, who can favorably affect sales and earnings, and members of the financial community, who can puff the company's stock and perhaps cause a run up in price. Local, who stands to gain personally from either occurrence, may have scheduled Exalted One to meet with either or both types. CEO will tell you if your presence is desired at such a meeting. If you are invited, be smart enough to understand that you are not there to do any talking. Leader is quite capable, and certainly very willing, to handle the talking chores by himself, thank you.

Suppress your shock when he begins to get carried away while discussing his company, going far beyond the facts. Give not the slightest indication of your dismay at the fantasies flowing from his lips. If you are among the accursed afflicted with showing true feelings by the expression on your face, either come up with a plausible excuse for not attending, or tune out completely. Speak only when his highness requests you to do so, and be damn sure you know what you are talking about when you do. Foot-in-mouth disease is often fatal.

Never elaborate on the comments of CEO. "If I had thought that should have been said, by God I would have said it."

Homeward bound. Don't mention how tired you are; rather, refer to your journey as an enriching and enjoyable experience. Let Number One lead the conversation. Answer his questions and give him information likely to enhance his opinion of you. Don't be modest. What you say you accomplished counts for more than what you actually accomplished. When Leader is not talking to you, be very busy reviewing your notes and writing your report of the trip. Just don't sit there staring out the window.

In your bye-bye to CEO be sure to include thanks for bringing you along. Tell him how much you enjoyed being with him and how much you learned from him. A bit fulsome? Yes. Effective? Bet your life on it.

CHAPTER 15

LET YOUR WORDS BE HEARD

To achieve potential, you must speak in public. The more you speak, the greater your chances of becoming a top executive. Getting yourself in front of audiences must be one of your first objectives.

At first don't concern yourself with either the quantity or quality of your audiences. Concentrate only on lining up speaking engagements and making sure that word of your appearances trickles up to your betters.

Get on a platform. Your company offers the best first forum. Volunteer your services at every opportunity. If you don't succeed, promote your speaking skills to outside groups. Clubs and civic groups are always searching for speakers (they need them to justify getting together for lunch).

More marketing (formerly sales) meetings are held than any other kind, so if you have some connection with marketing you stand a better chance of ending up on the speaker's platform.

Keep suggesting to the meeting planner how your appearance on the program can add zest and zing to the proceedings. Don't be disheartened if you are turned down several times. Persist in your efforts. Planner will either become convinced you will add something to the program or give in to be rid of you.

Some companies have program committees. Get appointed to the committee and put yourself on the program.

If your job is not directly associated with marketing, use one of the oldest bromides in the business world to put yourself at the podium: "The sales (now marketing) department isn't the entire company, but the entire company is the sales (marketing) department." Send a memo to the head of marketing pointing out the importance of your operation to the sales curve (it is not yet called marketing curve) and why all the marketing people should understand how you can help them—and how much you want to help them—increase sales.

Cozy up to the head of personnel and point out how you can add sparkle to a meeting of the company associates. If your firm has a speakers' bureau, get yourself appointed to it.

Make your speech effective. Once you are put on a program, work hard on making a good impression. Shove all other assignments aside and make the speech your top priority. For God's sake, don't just write it and read it. Burnish into your brain that just as actors do not read from a script in a play or movie, genuine role players do not read a speech.

In the beginning, you may not be able to solo without a script. Make soloing a goal to be reached quickly. The first impression you make as a speaker will likely be a lasting one, so even in your initial exposure, don't read your talk verbatim. Write it, then rewrite it until the words flow clearly and smoothly. Lots of rewriting will improve your talk and also enable you to recall more of your lines without looking at the text. To impress the hotshots, your speech needs at least several memorable phrases. If you can't think of any, steal some.

Don't try to memorize your talk. You will come off more like a robot than a dynamic leader rousing the troops to charge. You say you were a great memorizer in school? You have lost a lot of brain cells since those days. Your memory, even if it is quite good, can malfunction without notice, especially when you are in front of people you are trying to impress. Avoid the possibility of putting yourself through the torment of standing in front of an audience with mouth agape and eyes glazed, searching furiously and futilely for something to say.

While acquiring public speaking skills through on-the-job training, make sure you have some crutches handy in case you need them to keep from falling on your face. If you are convinced you will surely panic without a word-for-word text in front of you, highlight the most important passages with a yellow marker. Using this little trick will enable you to stray from the text to maintain some eye contact with your audience without being overwhelmed by fright at the prospect of losing your place. You can always read the highlighted parts.

Your next step is developing a rather full outline, then phasing into a skimpy one. Both steps will hasten the arrival of that glorious day when you ascend the podium with no written text in your hand, no outline in your pocket.

Capitalize fully on your liberation from a text or an outline. Move out from the lecturn. Wear a neck microphone as you prowl the stage to dramatize and flaunt your skills in pulling all those catchy words and fancy phrases from your head rather than from a piece of paper.

If your company provides a staff for preparing or assisting with the writing of talks, decline the offer of help. Your talk must be you—your humor, your timing, and your phrases (even if you didn't think of them first).

Some companies decree that all talks for a meeting be scripted by so-called specialists "to ensure continuity and consistency in communicating the desired message." Tell the ghosts you will faithfully follow the party line, but in your own way, as their words don't fit your mouth. And you will probably be telling the truth.

Do not limit your talk to words coming only from your own mouth. Employ as many tricky techniques as you can handle deftly. Be creative, but not corny. There is a hell of a big difference between the two. When giving someone else's opinion on a subject you are discussing, don't merely quote. Rather, walk to a tape recorder, push the play button, and let the expert do the telling. All the while the tape is playing, look out into the audience with a satisfied, but not smug, smile on your face. The second the speaker on the tape finishes, push the off button with a flourish, then resume your routine.

Using slides is OK, providing they are interesting and technically well done—requirements seldom met. Both slides and flip charts are susceptible to being deadly dull. Seldom can the numbers be read by anyone past the second row. Taking time to explain what the various colors and graphic symbols represent can make your presentation seem as long as the Bible tells us eternity will be. Slowly paced slide presentations are as unappealing as stale beer.

Star on a panel. About the only good feature of appearing as part of a panel discussion is that it beats not being on the program—but just barely. The big problem with panel discussions is that there is practically always one egotistical, selfish smart aleck who trys to hog the spotlight, dominate the discussion, talk louder than the others, and appear superior. Don't worry about it. Hog, dominate the discussion, talk louder than the others, and appear superior. That's just business, nothing personal intended.

To assist panel members in coordinating their talks, and to eliminate duplication, a dress rehearsal will probably be held. What you say and do at the rehearsal should bear little resemblance to what you intend to do and say. Stick to your script in rehearsal, read it word for word. Save your goodies for the real thing. Follow the moderator's instructions to the letter. Act almost diffident. Offer only one suggestion—that you be the first to speak.

As soon as the moderator introduces you, turn on like

a tiger. Animate, gesticulate, enthuse, and entertain. Soon your fellow panel members will be livid with rage. "That son of a bitch tricked us," they will say to themselves. All their focus will now be on you, rather than on what they are going to say. When their turns come, fluster will show on their faces, their mental disarray will be apparent. A more foolhardy type may switch from planned pitch and try to extemporize to match or top you. Don't sweat it. Extemporizer, being so distraught, will surely bomb.

Don't stop with your initial advantage. Stay on the attack. When your moderator tells you your time is up, say you have just one more very important point to make. Keep on talking until you have said all you want to say.

When the next panelist comes on, interrupt after two or three minutes with a comment or question. Do the same thing to the other panelists. When a panelist begins to come on particularly strong, interrupt several times. What about the ground rules agreed upon at rehearsal? That was rehearsal. This is the real performance, in the presence of those who determine your future.

Speak like an executive. Avoid making self-deprecating comments or overdoing the humility bit. All those who put themselves down before an audience while attempting to make a point literally broadcast that they do not have a very high opinion of themselves. A small amount of jabbing yourself may assist you in empathizing with your audience, but be very careful not to play the role of fool.

Nor should you come on as a clown. Don't wear a costume or extreme attire to prove a point. A straw hat is permitted when announcing a "Summer Sellabration" (every company seems to have one at some time) but even then only if everyone in the audience is wearing one. Women role players should never agree to wear risqué attire, even while performing in a skit. That's asking for the wrong kind of attention.

Speak on other stages. Should all your efforts to get on the program at one of your company's meetings be unsuccessful, don't despair. Work on having your words heard by local clubs and organizations.

Here's how to put yourself on local platforms: If your specialized field is of general interest to a group of people with the varied backgrounds found in the memberships of civic and service clubs, prepare a talk on that subject. Women playing executive roles should not speak only to women's clubs or talk on "the women's point of view." Your speaking should focus on the big picture, not just part of it.

Chances are, a speech on your specialty will be a bit too esoteric for the knife-and-fork folks, but don't let that keep you off the platform. Develop two talks which are unfailingly popular with joiners: a speech on the glories of the American free enterprise system and an inspiring motivational message on how one can reach all one's goals.

"But," you may be saying, "I am neither an economist nor a psychologist." Forget it. You are in business. Many psychologists and economists are in academe or on radio talk shows. You have experience, which counts for a lot more than vague theories untested in the arena of real life. Develop a talk on each subject.

Extolling the virtues of American business. Getting across these points assures a standing ovation from your audience:

- Stress the importance of the organization to which you are speaking.
- Declare that the American free enterprise system has produced the highest living standard in the world (and you'll be telling the truth).
- Praise hard work and damn indolence.
- Emphasize that success involves taking risks, and the greater the risk, the greater the potential rewards. "The only true security is that enjoyed by those confined to jails."
- Explain why handouts are harmful to those who receive them as well as to those who pay for them. "There's no such thing as a free lunch."

- Quote Adam Smith, Milton Friedman, John Stuart Mill, and William F. Buckley, Jr.
- Decry the "economic illiteracy" afflicting an appalling number of the American citizenry.
- Call for less government intervention and more freedom in the marketplace. Be especially harsh on OSHA and EEOC.
- Urge your audience to become "politically involved."
- Conclude with a plea that everyone in attendance make known to their senators and representatives their views on the government's intrusion into the private sector.

Deliver a motivating message.

- Wear a neck microphone, walk across the stage, even into the audience. Never look at a note.
- Attract attention with an unusual gimmick such as an alarm wrist watch that goes off when your allotted time expires.
- Proclaim "To be enthusiastic, you must act enthusiastically." Practice what you preach by jumping over a chair—but don't trip over your mike cord. (Better bring your own chair to make sure you can hurdle it successfully.)
- Quote the gurus of positive thinking, such as Dr. Norman Vincent Peale and W. Clement Stone.
- Use lots of clichés and bromides. Be sure to include old faithful: "You may not be what you think you are, but what you think, you are."
- Stress the importance of setting goals, high ones.
- Urge best efforts by emphasizing "More people rust out than wear out."
- Ask questions that require "great" in the answer. There is something inherently stirring in the word "great."
- Be a power figure by using a blackboard.
- Quote the Bible and always cite chapter and verse.
- Assure your audience they can achieve much more than they presently are "if they want to enough."
- Talk rapid fire; use lots of gestures; pause for effect; repeat key phrases.

- Charge up the audience so they are ready to run out of the room when you are finished.

When starting out on the stump, keep your talks to no more than twenty minutes. As you gain platform experience you will learn to gauge the listening capacity of your audience and sense when to turn off. Avoid extended speeches before you have established a reputation as a great speaker.

Capitalize on your speaking. When talking to outside groups you are wise to mention the name of your company and your CEO. Emphasize that your appearance is made possible by His Grace's firm commitment to propagating the views you are expressing. The purpose of this little ploy is, of course, to inform your audience to whom and where messages of praise of your performance should be sent.

When the letters start coming in, Leader will send them on to you with a notation expressing his personal thanks and congratulations for doing such a fine job. If enough of these letters arrive, assuming his secretary lets him see them before she sends them to a P. R. type to acknowledge for him, his curiosity will be piqued to the point that he asks for your personnel file to learn more about you. He may even come down from the mountain to congratulate you in person and visit with you. If he doesn't deign to descend, arrange to meet him under somewhat favorable circumstances. Gain entrance to the promised land by using the pretext of thanking him for his thoughtful comments on the letters he received about your speeches. In either situation, let him know you are ready to carry the company's banner to any podium he wants to send you.

Become a recognized speaker. If CEO doesn't do anything about getting you off the local knife-and-fork circuit, develop your own devices for taking your message across the country. If you belong to a national trade association, send the program chair copies of the laudatory letters from satisfied listeners. Persuade your friends at your company to recommend you to the program chairs of their associations. Always tell them that your appearing on the program will be good for both the firm and their standing in the associations.

As soon as you are invited to appear on the program of a national group, get to work immediately on your speech, even if your appearance is months away. While developing your comments keep in mind that some in your audience can give you a better job in a bigger company, and will if you turn on hotshot's hot button.

When speaking to the association to which you belong, set a secondary goal. Impress the lords to the point they will designate you as a comer and anoint you as an officer, an act leading to your becoming president of the association.

If you speak to the association to which you belong, you will receive some special attention, but not much. When you speak to other business associations, you'll be given genuine celebrity treatment. Very likely a member of the program committee, perhaps even the chair, will meet your plane and whisk you away to the hotel. No fussing around with waiting for taxis or buses for guest speakers. Your host will give you a packet containing the meeting program, a booklet showing the best restaurants and watering holes, a tablet encased in an attractive cover bearing the logo of the association, a ballpoint pen for notetaking, and a roster of attendees. Check the roster carefully to determine if there are any people present who are worth impressing.

Your real reward is the badge you receive. No ordinary badge this, for from it hangs a ribbon, usually red but sometimes white, proclaiming in large block letters "Guest Speaker." All who see that coveted trapping recognize immediately that you are not just another attendee come to listen, but rather a speaker come to inform.

Probably your host will stick with you throughout the meeting, ministering to your every need. Make the most of your celebrity. If you speak at the end of the meeting, arrive at the opening in order to "get a feeling for the audience and to tie my remarks to what has been said before." If you speak early in the meeting, stay the entire time because "so many people wanted to talk to me about the ideas I presented that to have left early would have produced negative attitudes toward, rather than positive benefits for, the company."

Most associations give each speaker a memento, such as a thermometer, barometer, or pen set, each appropriately inscribed. Be sure to display all your speaking trophies in a prominent place in your office to provide further evidence of your platform skills and the wide demand for them.

Never take money, not a dime, for your speaking. Your salary comes from your company, as do your expenses of attending the meeting. You are there to puff your firm, not stuff your pockets. The leading lights will take a dim view of your stashing some cash for services the company is paying for.

Recognize that speaking is a means to an end—greater visibility to produce a higher position—rather than an end in itself. Many companies, practically all large ones, have at least one person on staff whose only assignment is giving speeches. It's not a bad job, providing you don't mind living out of suitcases and don't aspire to the executive suite. Once a professional speaker, always a professional speaker. Your sword of Damocles is overexposure. When organizations stop asking for your services, expect your boss to take you to lunch to talk in glowing terms about the glories of early retirement—for you, not him.

CHAPTER 16

SOCIALIZE WITH CAUTION

Some companies foster intramural fraternizing, some frown on the practice, and others don't give a damn either way. If fraternizing is encouraged or tacitly permitted, fraternize. But when you do, beware of the pitfalls. They are many and deep.

When spouses are involved in the fraternizing, both the number and the depth of the pitfalls increase considerably. A wife or husband "who doesn't fit in with the group" or is honest and disdains role playing can blow up a career. Better to risk being tagged "uppity" than to hazard having your career sabotaged by your spouse.

Rubbing and bending elbows with your peers. If at all possible, be a friend to all but a close friend to none. The major factor in your decision should be that which applies in all business situations—conforming to what the hotshots expect of you. If your peers fraternize, you should, too. Also accept the fact that all such encounters are strictly no-win deals, for what you do and say can and will be used against you. Prepare for each intramural encounter on the basis that some bastard is out to get you. Frequently you will be right.

By conforming you are confirming you are a team player and that you and your fellow executives form one, big, happy family. Fool them but not yourself. Misconduct, real or imagined, deducts brownie points from your performance appraisal.

Pray fervently to the good Lord above that you never get trapped into regularly scheduled activities with your peer group, such as round-robin dinners or bridge games, or tennis or golf outings and the like. The wise one who coined what has now become an old saying "Familiarity breeds contempt" probably got the idea attending an intramural social event.

Peer parties, always dangerous, have become even more tricky and scary as a result of women's coming into the executive ranks. No longer are men found congregated in one group and women in another. For now some executives are women, and some of the spouses are men.

Women in executive roles should be cordial to the wives present but should spend most of their time socializing with peers. To act like just another woman gives credence to the plaint of at least some of the men: "She belongs at home, not in an office."

Single women executives should anticipate being monitored especially closely by most of the wives, and expect to receive some sharp looks and perhaps a cutting remark or two. Remember that some women still believe "If she were a real woman, she'd be raising kids and keeping house."

It is unwise for women executives to host a peer party at home. To do so requires performing a delicate balancing act between competent executive and charming hostess, not an easy task. Those forced to have their peer groups for dinner should never cook and/or serve the meal. Have the affair catered or let husband (or boyfriend) barbecue steaks or hamburgers. Unattached women can at least hire a cook and waiter.

Special problems confront women executives with any of the following types of husbands: blowhards who know the answers before the questions are asked; insecures who want to spend the whole evening proving that their positions in their companies are more important than those of anyone else present; would-be Lotharios. Women bearing any of these burdens should accept invitations to peer parties only when their husbands are out of town or "abed ailing."

Husbands of women role players have no easy time either. They must listen to shoptalk as if they enjoy it. They need not be macho men to resent being identified as their wives' husbands. Those playing the role of "house husband" had better have very thick skins.

Male executives and their wives may also have problems. Men must be concerned that their spouses act like ladies at all times and not try to play the role of sex kitten or gossip columnist. Wives must be alert to the possibility of husbands' sinking their ship of dreams by saying the wrong thing to the wrong person or conducting themselves in "unbusinesslike" ways.

Both executives and spouses must be especially careful of what they say at peer parties. The trick to turn is to obtain as much information as possible without revealing anything of importance.

Try to capitalize on the opportunity to pick up juicy tidbits flowing from tongues loosened by liquor. Pick up your ears as soon as you hear someone begin a statement with a plea for secrecy, such as "Understand that this is strictly between you and me." Nod your head to demonstrate that you wouldn't think of saying a word to anyone, then suck up the gossip.

Be smarter than your associates. Never reveal gossip or give inside information to anyone, regardless of how vehemently they vow to keep their lips sealed. They won't, but will probably add some embellishments of their own in the retelling. Before speaking a word at a peer party, measure it on the basis of "Can this damage my career if it gets back to the powers that be that I am the source of it?"

Drinking too much can be a big problem—not just your or your spouse's overimbibing, but that of others present, too. Almost always at least one screw-up will get a snootful, then become a bit amorous, beginning with asking for a little "kissy poo" and working up to some grabbing of private property. To be the love object of a libido fired to fever pitch by too many martinis, manhattans, or whatever is to incur automatically the wrath of your spouse. ("You must have said or done something to bring it on.") If miscreant is boss's spouse, consider yourself incinerated.

Avoid amorous ones like the plague they are. When one asks for a kissy poo, plead strep throat. In case of boss's spouse, declare double pneumonia.

It is entirely possible you will meet a couple at an intramural party you find quite likable and whose chemistry immediately clicks with yours and your spouse's. You can be genuine friends. You are convinced they will keep confidential any comments you make about the company and the executives. Go slowly, very slowly here. Status is much thicker than friendship. If one of the two of you passes up someone else, that is cause for celebration. If one of you passes up the other, a once warm friendship may go into the deep freeze.

Conducting yourself at the club. Should your company provide club memberships for those reaching a predesignated executive level, your problems related to socializing with company associates will be compounded considerably when you reach that level. The only clubs open to you are those which do not use bloodlines as the standard of eligibility, unless, of course, you are among the few who can pass the blood test. If you aren't located in a very large city, your choice of clubs will be quite limited. In any event, you will probably be unable to find a club offering at least some prestige which doesn't have any members from your company.

Select the club with members from your firm with whom you are reasonably compatible and which is likely to accept your application for membership. Being rejected by any country club is akin to being sent into exile. If there is a skeleton in your closet which might be shaken loose into the light of day by the club's membership committee's investigation, either don't apply or seek out a club which takes anyone with enough money to pay the initiation fee.

Once you have been accepted for membership, other club members from your company will feel duty-bound to invite you to participate in club activities with them and to introduce you to other club members to help you adjust to the high altitude. Accept their offer, but tell them you don't want to interfere with their regular routine and that you want to get into a group of your own as soon as possible. Do just that as soon as you can without appearing snooty about it.

Both you and your spouse should move slowly in participating in the social activities of your new club. Do not flutter around the bar and dining room as if you were social butterflies. You can be certain that every action of yours will be under close and constant scrutiny by the established club members of your company. Be equally certain that judgments will be made as to whether your conduct at the club meets accepted standards for those deserving to be designated top executive material.

Never invite nonmembers from your company to your club. Make no exceptions to this rule. Exposing nonmembers to the good life lived by club members will cause them to come through the experience either full of the natives-are-restless syndrome or with illusions of grandeur, thinking they ought to belong to a country club. Both of these attitudes are completely understandable. . .and totally unacceptable. Avoid putting yourself in the position of sowing seeds of insurrection among the working class.

It is perfectly OK to invite members of other clubs to yours and to accept invitations from them. Important side benefits accrue from going to other clubs. You enhance your status considerably by knowing and discussing what other clubs offer.

Associating with underlings. Use much caution in fraternizing with people who report to you either directly or through your assistants. On rare occasions it is OK to accept an invitation to a social event hosted by a lesser. Keep your acceptances to an irreducible minimum to spare both you and your spouse much aggravation.

As the ranking executive present at such events, you will be smiled at and fawned over throughout the ordeal. The lesser lights and their spouses will go all out to impress you and your spouse. Don't scorn them for their obsequiance. Rather, think back to what you did and said to earn your present position. Accept the attention and adulation you are receiving for the acts of role playing they are. Above all, never delude yourself into thinking that any of their words or actions are sincere.

Being performed for, rather than having to perform, does have redemptive features. You can be very cool throughout. About the only error you can make in such a situation is to let your hair down to prove to one and all that you are not really a son of a bitch but in truth just one of the proletariat. Top executives do not regard proletarians as executive material.

Getting smashed at the party is one sure way, but certainly not the only one, to lower your level of conduct to that of the great unwashed. Becoming involved in a poker game, or heaven forbid, a crap game, is the absolute nadir. Discussing office gossip is to be avoided. By nature, underlings are reluctant to reveal indiscretions of an overling. They feel perfectly free, however, to quote what you said, or as is frequently the case, what they thought you said.

Try hard to eliminate the possibility of encountering the many problems associated with the dreary chore of entertaining underlings. One good way is to pass the word among your troops that you have always developed your social friends outside the company to broaden your base of association and to add to your knowledge of general business. Circulate that line widely to get off the hook for both extending invitations to, and accepting them from, your lessers.

If you have been indiscreet about accepting invitations to parties hosted by underlings, not to give a pay-back party would be gauche. Get the ordeal over with as soon as you can, then resolve firmly never to be so stupid or masochistic as to put yourself through such a tribulation again.

Invite only underlings who hosted parties you attended and those who are, and will continue to be, useful to you in securing a higher position. Under no circumstances include your peers and superiors. Most would feel obliged to accept, but all would resent being forced to mingle with the masses.

Whenever possible, entertain underlings outside your home. If you must use your home as the stage for this presentation, you and your spouse should prepare yourselves to have your underlings inspect your furniture, decor, china, crystal, silverware, even your brands of booze with a microscopic eye. They will check your carpeting for plushness and any signs of wear. Do not become too irritated at their actions. It is only natural for them to want to see how they can expect to live when they succeed in getting your job. The more prosperous you appear, the more they will be motivated to undercut you.

Avoid office post-mortem discussions of your party. When someone thanks you for the "lovely, fun party," respond with a curt "thank you" and start talking business. Keep telling yourself: "That's over and done with and by God there won't be any more."

Hobnobbing with overlings. Accept all invitations extended by your betters. Invite higher-ups very infrequently and only when you are ninety-nine percent certain of an acceptance.

When a very higher-up, i.e., Numbers One through Three, requests the honour (seldom do any of them use plain old honor) of your and your spouse's presence, don't get carried away with the fantasy that a big promotion is in the works. First scan the guest list. If it is not readily accessible, obtain it from your host's secretary under the pretext that it is for your spouse's information.

A man who is the lowest ranking one on the list should flush from his mind any thoughts of a promotion and get his feet back on the ground quickly. His being included in the festivities does not necessarily mean that he has been invited for the purpose of serving as butt boy, but it is certainly a strong indication. It is quite understandable why Big Man needs someone to "look after things" for him. If his definition of "looking after things" includes taking care of the guest's coats, tending bar, and sticking around to clean up, so be it. It is quite unlikely a female executive will be asked to play the role of charwoman. Most leading players are too chivalrous for that.

Anyone invited to a hotshot's party for the purpose of "looking after things" must concentrate solely on "looking after things." Mingling with the other guests can be done only when nothing needs to be looked after, which will be seldom. One must make it perfectly clear to wife that she has been invited for the same reason. Before the party starts, wife should be made to understand what she is to do. This lesson is known officially as "understanding and keeping thy place." If wife mentions that she is not a maid, she should be informed that she might end up as one if she blows this assignment.

If the number of invitees from your peer group exceeds the number of people required to "look after things" for even a first-class party, a promotion may indeed be involved. The party's true purpose could be for hotshot to obtain the opinions of friends in high places in other companies on the relative degree of social grace possessed by each one being screened. Certainly the ability to handle oneself gracefully with high-society types is an important measure of executive suite potential. Spouses, too, must be redolent with social grace.

Of course, there is no way to determine for certain if this party is in reality the calling together of many for the anointing of one. Do not dismiss the possibility until you have thoroughly evaluated the circumstances surrounding the invitation. Review the guest list again. If a number of those you regard as rivals are included, chances are quite good that the big moment for which you have waited so long and impatiently is at hand. If guests from outside the company include a number of prestigious individuals whose judgment is highly regarded by the host, chances are excellent this is it. If one of the outside guests is a management consultant or a head hunter, all chance is eliminated. Your big moment has surely arrived.

Whether you are certain or only suspect that the party is merely subterfuge for a tryout, prepare diligently for the big occasion, but don't overtrain. You must act as if you are there to enjoy the frolic with the bigwigs and haven't the slightest idea of what is really going on. Being obvious in your efforts to impress the critics is to assure your receiving a bad review. Socialites consider pushy types to be pariahs.

Learn as much as you can about guests from outside the company. Probe on the sly so that word doesn't get out that you are presumptuous enough to be investigating people of such high standing. With the information obtained you should be able to carry on a somewhat intelligent conversation with each of them.

Let the blue bloods from the outside world do most of the talking, if they are so inclined, as they probably are. Good listeners always make excellent impressions. This one night take a tuck in your ego and suppress your natural inclination to talk about yourself and your interests. This is no time to act naturally.

Should you be unable to uncover any clues on the personal interests of the guests who are sitting as your judges, don't fret too much. Praising conservative politicians and causes should impress any business leader worthy of the name.

Many pillars of the business community share an acute sensitivity to the slightest inference that they got where they are through family connections. Avoid all references to fathers, grandfathers, or other family members presently or previously connected with their companies. If you don't know the family connections, don't ask. You can't err by acting as if they reached their present position of prominence entirely on their own.

Make sure that your costume for the big event is neat and attractive, but not gaudy. Above all, don't wear anything even slightly frayed or not of obvious high quality.

Train for the test so that your poise and savoir faire will reach peak form on that very day. Be calm, at least externally. Nervousness can cause you to spill a drink on Big Man's fancy carpet.

Don't smoke! Even if you are a chain smoker, do without the noxious weed the three or so hours your act will be scrutinized. Two drinks are the absolute maximum, one a hell of a lot safer. Hope that your rivals are more reckless.

Avoid giving any indication that you are checking reactions to your statements to keep from appearing insecure. Before engaging any of the high falutings in conversation, make sure your mouth is connected to your mind, then express your thoughts with confidence and in a few words. Be sure to bring all of your charm with you to the party. You'll need every drop of it.

Lunching with CEO. Some leaders prefer to select top executives through tête-à-tête sessions with each candidate. Don't expect the confrontation to originate with number One's calling you to his office and asking you lots of questions. He is much too suave for that. It is more likely he will invite you to lunch, usually on short notice to give you less time to prepare. When CEO's secretary phones to ask if you are free to dine with The Boss at the Got Rocks Club, know that a one-on-one audition is nigh, and that the lunch serves a business, not social purpose.

Be at the appointed place five minutes before the appointed time. Chances are, Number One will be ten minutes late (always being pressed for time is an important part of his act), but the slight possibility exists that he may be on time or even a little bit early. To keep CEO waiting is to ensure that you won't be the one selected for the promotion.

If you ride in the company's limo, be very nonchalant. If you are asked to drive, use more caution than you ordinarily do. If you go by taxi, give your destination to the driver and speak not another word to him. Answer the driver's questions with grunts.

Exalted One is apt to begin the conversation by saying that he has received a number of favorable comments on your job performance, and because the company's future is inexorably bound to the quality of its executive staff, especially younger members, he wants to become better acquainted with you. Thus beginneth the inquisition.

His questioning will be much more intensive than the grilling he gave you on your first trip with him. He may cover some of the same ground, but in much more detail. Make sure all your answers agree with the information in your personnel file. Sometimes being consistent is more important than being honest. This is one of the times.

Let CEO set the luncheon pace. If he recommends an item as being especially tasty, order it. Pass the cocktail, even if your host has one. If he pulls the old "I'll have one if you have one" play, block him out with "I'll have a Perrier and lemon." The Perrier bit will surely impress him.

If he is a slow eater, you eat slowly, too. If he inhales his food, cleaning his plate before you can clear your throat, eat as quickly as you can without giving yourself a gas attack. Belching and burping will not endear you to your leader.

After the inquisition and lunch, he will shift to a discussion of the company to elicit your views on operations. Here are some likely questions and appropriate responses:

Q: What do you think of the company's overall performance?

A: It's very good.

Q: What kind of company is it to work for?

A: The best I have experienced, or for that matter, heard about.

Q: What do you think is our greatest strength?

A: We have many, but as you have asked for one I'll cite our five-year strategic plan which clearly outlines where we are going and how we are going to get there.

Q: What is our biggest weakness?

A: (You must not er or ah on this one.) I don't think we have a big one. I hear more grumbling about shipping procedures than anything else, but I don't believe we have any serious problems anywhere. (Shipping is always a good target as it is highly unlikely the person in charge has any standing in the hierarchy. If your company doesn't have a shipping department, give a soft jab to an operation whose standing is similar to that of a shipping department in firms which have one.)

Q: If you were given the authority to change one operation in the company any way you wanted, how would you change it?

A: (A truthful answer would be: "Have someone else sitting in this chair answering your damn trick questions.") As I am one who concentrates on positives rather than negatives, I will have to ruminate (say "think on it" if "ruminate" may be a bit of a problem for him) for a moment. (Search your mind quickly to make sure you don't give an answer which steps on his toes, even slightly.) I see no need for or desirability of even one major change. But if I were assigned to make one, I would immediately put in place a plan for clearing out the dead wood from the sales force and replacing them with young tigers. (Such a proposal is appropriate only if you are not involved in marketing [sales]. To bad mouth your own operation even slightly is disloyalty per se. If you are in marketing, suggest that the dead-wood engineers be replaced by more imaginative ones.)

On your return trip to the office, thank Peerless Leader for the nice lunch and be lavish in your praise of Got Rocks Club. Sit back and wait for the jury of one to bring in its verdict.

Attending company parties. Practically all companies hold some type of event at which the hoi polloi mingle with the highbrows—be it picnic, dance, Christmas party, etc. Christmas parties seem to be the most popular. So much has been written and spoken factually, fictionally, and facetiously about the pitfalls inherent in yuletide office gatherings that even neophyte role players realize they are dynamite which can explode a career.

Some companies hold more than one affair a year. Most invite all office associates. Seldom is the working class, i.e., those paid by the hour, included.

For clerical types, the great unwashed, and their spouses,

company parties are the highlight of their social season. Just the thought of being able to go to a swanky hotel or restaurant they can't afford on their own fills them with excitement and exhilaration. For a few fleeting hours, they are close to the fancy people they usually see only from afar.

Executives and their spouses regard company parties as insufferably boring, never enjoyed, barely endured. Why, then, do they go? They go because they are not stupid. They know that their presence is not merely requested, that it is required. Attendance at company parties is similar to semi-annual visits to the dentist. Both are painful, but for making a good appearance.

When attending a social function of the company you must not indicate in the slightest the inner pain racking both your body and your soul. Fraternize with all of your troops, meeting all the spouses and saying all the meaningless words said to people one must appear to enjoy but with whom one shares no common interests. Certainly the experience is distasteful, but your mission is to display the humanity of the corporation. Turn in a good performance.

Drink moderately, of course, and dine with your troops, not your peers or betters. Give your undivided attention to your underlings for a couple of hours. There are other times and other places to mix with equals and overlings. The party won't last forever, it'll only seem that way.

Socializing with your boss. In a nutshell, keep your personal relations with your boss to the minimum required for maintaining good relations. As women's advancement to the executive ranks has been a relatively recent development, the simple fact is that the vast majority of executives are men. Consequently, the actions of both male superiors and subordinates are more clearly patterned and, therefore, more predictable. So this advice on relating socially to the boss applies mainly in cases of males working for males.

But female executives should be active socially. Not being regarded as "one of the boys" is a high hurdle all female role players must jump. When the boss invites you and some of your peers to have an after-hours drink, accept the offer.

As a general rule, well-adjusted and secure bosses have friends consisting of their economic and social equals. Bosses do not regard help as either an economic or social equal, so don't expect the boss to socialize with you.

Don't invite your boss to dinner at your home or to attend social events with you. Always wait until you have worked for a boss at least six months before trying to become cozy. In that time you will be able to gauge better how such an invitation will help your cause. If you have been to the boss's home, etiquette requires your reciprocating. If you invite people from outside the company to the pay-back affair, include only those likely to impress the boss.

If your home is nicer or more fancily furnished than the boss's, never invite, regardless of etiquette demands. The law of survival always takes precedence over manners. Sure, the boss has heard about your fancy pad, in fact has probably driven by at dusk to sneak a peek. But never let him examine it microscopically. He won't like being second to you in anything. Mrs. Boss may accuse him of being a poor provider. Jealous or nagged bosses are not ardent boosters.

Pray fervently that neither your boss nor his wife is so maladjusted and insecure as to feel the need to hold court frequently for their retinue of lackeys. Should either boss or wife insist on being fawned over, recognize that they consider your time to be their time, and as long as you work for boss accept the fact that you are expected to jump through the hoops they hold as if you enjoy it.

CHAPTER 17

PULL YOURSELF TO THE TOP

"Someday you are going to be a top executive in this company" is a comment a leading light makes to anyone regarded as a comer. Your mission is to make someday become now. If you have labored for some time in the vineyard and have heard no words or seen no signs pointing toward your elevation to a top position, you had better start making things happen.

You can accelerate your rise to stardom in a number of ways. Unfortunately, none of them is free of risk of backfire. Don't let that stop you from trying. Getting to the top isn't a game for the fainthearted.

Hitch to a hotshot. Obviously, CEO will tug you faster and farther than anyone else in the company, but he is hard to get. Chances are, his hitch is already loaded with leading lights seeking his pull in being anointed his successor.

If Number One's hitch is full, concentrate on endearing yourself to the higher-up generally regarded as the heir apparent. It is even permissible to become the protege of several top executives, providing they are reasonably compatible, at least on the surface. But proceed very cautiously in making dual hitches. One strong hitch is much better than two or more tentative ones—as long as you were prescient enough to have picked the one with the most pull.

If a son or son-in-law is associated with the firm, you should hitch to him only after he has been anointed as Crown Prince and while, to use a figure of speech, he is working his way to the top. That's because there are always a few diehards who cling to the hope, against overwhelming odds, that son will live off his dividends and inheritance, join a religious cult, or become one of those rarest of princes who seeks to become king on his merits in another firm. The diehards do not merely dislike son or son-in-law of Number One—they despise him. Son's presence on the scene has demolished their dream, secretly held but fervently clung to, of someday becoming CEO. Son's coming upon the scene has transformed these once fierce foes into strong allies. Their common cause is to make life as difficult as possible for son until the anointing as successor actually occurs.

Father CEO must necessarily limit his intervention on son's behalf to major questions. God knows, son creates enough major questions. The confederacy of the frustrated can be counted on to do a first-class hatchet job on anyone son recommends for promotion, so don't become too friendly with son until he is officially designated as successor to CEO.

If hitch of anointed son is already full, either reconcile yourself to the fact that your chances of becoming a top executive in this company are quite remote or start looking for another. Above all, don't alienate him. Many a promising career has been cut short by "son stroke."

Daughters of Top Stars can also be effective hitches, providing they intend to stay on the scene and become leaders in their own right. But hitching to someone who will soon be gone literally leaves you in the lurch. Although women are making progress in business and will likely pick up the pace in the future, the fact remains that men still have practically all the power. So female aspirants to top spots are wise to hitch to a male leading light unless the company has that rare exception—a woman at or near the top.

Once you have selected a power to hitch to, make sure the fit is as firm as possible. If your hitch is your immediate boss who isn't in the management level just below CEO and Number Two, you haven't hitched high enough. Raise your sights. Go for your boss's boss.

Recognize that a person with power is usually not content with having one protege on hitch. Power House has put on one hell of an act and endured lots of guff to become a leading executive and feels entitled to be fawned and fussed over by as many as possible.

Quickly acquaint yourself with the likes and dislikes of your hitch. Also discover his idiosyncracies. You must learn to think as he thinks, act as he acts. You don't need to be his clone, but you should come very close.

Discovering whether your hitch is methods- or results-oriented merits top priority. As most executives focus on the how, chances are excellent your hitch concentrates on methods. If hitch turns out to be a results man, unhitch quickly and look for a methods man.

Pay particular attention to your hitch's style of memo writing. If he writes in narrative form, do likewise. If he employs the outline technique, so should you. It is not necessary, however, to emulate his tendencies to use a convoluted style of expression or to ignore rules of grammar. Hotshots tend to be more forgiving of themselves than they are of others.

The trick to turn with your hitch is to mirror his actions and echo his words without appearing to do so. Ignore the kidding you receive from your peers, accepting it as merely more of the pygmies kicking at the heels of the giants. If you are so obvious in aping your hero that your act subjects you to ridicule by your underlings as well as peers, you had better polish your performance. Leading lights do not like to be surrounded by clowns.

As your relationship with hitch becomes closer, both your salary and standing in the show will increase rapidly and significantly. So will the price you pay. Your time becomes hitch's time. An invitation from him to a social event is not merely an invitation, it is a command. Your home phone will ring whenever he feels the need for your services, or merely wants to talk to you. Some of his calls will probably come at ungodly hours. He may call you off the tennis court or golf course or out of the swimming pool to talk to you. He may phone you at a party you are attending to summon you to an emergency meeting at his home. Likely it is not a real emergency, but if he thinks it is, so should you.

Hitch may even call you on a holiday morning, ask you to come to a meeting at his home in the afternoon, then let out a big hah, hah, hah. This little joke may appear to be the end product of a fine sense of humor, but it reinforces unmistakably the master–servant relationship.

What price glory? You are now learning the price is quite high, and sometimes downright degrading. Swallow your pride and persist in keeping your eye on your goal. Console yourself that your servant role will be completed someday. Incidentally, if hitch isn't kidding about the holiday afternoon meeting, tell him to stuff it.

One of your most important duties is to serve as hitch's eyes and ears. It would be most unseemly for a leading player to snoop around and pump for the latest gossip and hottest rumors. He has a legitimate need to know what is going on in the company to be able to protect his own interests. As his interests are your interests, gather the information joyfully. Give hitch all the information you glean and don't filter it too finely. Allow him to determine the relative importance of the tidbits you hear or overhear. Juicy morsels about hitch's rivals will be especially welcome.

Be faithful in your fealty to your hitch—as long as he is in ascendancy. At first rumor of his impending fall, loosen the hitch by cooling the relationship, at least the visible parts of it. If hitch does fall from grace, unhitch immediately. Protégés of the deposed face dismal futures.

Hope the cut is clean, i.e., hitch is fired outright. Then he will not be around to remind you constantly of your serious, probably disastrous error in judgment. Hitch's complete removal from the scene will also make it easier for you to play Judas by disavowing any allegiance to him.

Dig former hitch at every opportunity. Be especially cutting in your comments to his major rival, the one probably responsible for putting the dagger into him or persuading someone else to do it. Try diligently to convey the relief you feel in no longer having to be associated with the bastard.

Accept the fact that chances are you won't fool the bigwigs. Immediately get busy on prettying your resume and circulating it widely. Contact all the head hunters you know. Avoid making any long-term commitments.

As many CEOs are unwilling to desecrate their holy hands with the blood of a once close associate, former hitch will probably remain with the company. Fallen will be the last to accept the fact that his power has been unplugged. In his blindness to reality he will expect the same unstinting loyalty you gave him when it was to your advantage to give it. The selfish bastard will presume that you will feed him more information now that his official sources have become dry holes. He can't just sit there and stare out the window all day long. He needs to talk to someone. Make sure that someone isn't you. You can be certain all of your contacts with broken-down hitch will be monitored closely by those on high.

In picking a star to hitch to, you are playing a high stakes game. Win, and someday you may become Number One, complete with private jet, chauffeured limo, and a congo line of sycophants. Lose, and at the minimum you are stuck forever in your present job. More likely you will be out on your ass. Hitching is truly a case of being right and soaring, being wrong and sinking.

Impress Mrs. CEO. Don't laugh. For indeed, it is a fact that making a very favorable impression on Mrs. Number One can cause her to try to pull you all the way to the top. But getting her to want to do that is certainly not easy.

Only truly exceptional role players should even consider selecting this route, ones especially skilled in making and maintaining good impressions.

In deciding whether or not your leader's wife can be helpful in convincing him to turn over to you his power and the keys to his fancy office and the private privy adjoining it, be guided by CEO's age. If you are considerably younger than Exalted One, better forget Mrs. CEO. You'll be too young to assume the throne when he abdicates or is overthrown. Of one thing you can be certain—wife of new CEO will not be impressed by the fact that old lady CEO thought you were hot stuff. It is more likely she will dislike your act only because her predecessor liked it.

Save your energy involved in trying to impress her if a son, daughter, or son-in-law is waiting in the wings to be called to center stage. (It is highly unlikely she would assist a daughter-in-law.) Also pay close attention to her track record with her favorites. Has she been faithful or fickle? If in the past she has selected others for special attention and later began to ignore them for one whim or another, seek another source of pull. She will probably drop you, too. Such a fall leaves permanent scars.

If she is presently sponsoring someone, forget her as a potential booster. You must become the favorite to cause her to want to take you to the top.

Other factors, crucial ones in deciding whether or not to take the distaff route are her degree of interest in company affairs and the amount of influence she wields with her roommate. Quite rare is the mogul's wife who manifests outwardly the slightest indication of interest. Even rarer is one who on the inside isn't full to overflowing with such interest. If she is one of the very few who displays outwardly her desire to run things, don't waste your time on her. The sweet, demure "I really don't know anything about business" type makes the best booster. Behind the closed doors of the mansion Mr. and Mrs. CEO call home, she is probably as sharp as a tack and hard as a steel bar.

To attract and retain her attention, you and your spouse must be perceived by her as "charming," not bright, not competent, not aggressive, not articulate, not stylish. You may have a little problem here because charm, like beauty, is in the eye of the beholder. What is charm to one may be strictly no class to another. Observe closely how she expresses herself to get a better handle on what she regards as charming.

Being judged charming usually requires displaying culture and couth in large quantities. Even if Mrs. CEO was not born with these sterling qualities, she has had to acquire them in large amounts to survive in the heady atmosphere her husband's success has thrust her. Simply because she was raised on a pig farm in Illinois and you came from a corn patch in Iowa doesn't mean that referring to your shared bucolic backgrounds assures instant rapport. She may regard you as an unreconstructed hick or resent your bringing up her humble beginnings. A role player must understand that growing in one's role frequently requires growing away from one's past.

Individuals in high-profile positions, i.e., those whose work is seen and analyzed by a significant number of people both within and outside the company, are making an impression on Mrs. CEO whether or not they realize it. As she listens to, watches, or reads the advertising, reports, or other company material, she makes value judgments on each which she freely expresses to CEO.

Results produced by heads of operating divisions are examined thoroughly by Mrs. Number One. Her interest in these numbers is certainly understandable. Profits determine the amount of CEO's salary, bonus, and dividends on stock which she has to spend.

Heads of operating divisions and those in high-profile positions should recognize that some of the criticisms coming from the lips of CEO may very well have originated in the mind of his sweet, demure, kindly wife. If his current opinion on a particular subject contradicts one previously expressed, don't immediately assume he has changed his mind, for it may very well be that his mind was changed for him by the lady who shares the same roof and perhaps bed with him.

Kowtowing to her every whim will surely leave a bad taste in your mouth. Gargle three times a day until you realize kowtowing is simply part of your act in getting a bigger role and that making favorable impressions on her as frequently as you can will give you the boost you need.

Become an industry guru. Once you become highly regarded by occupiers of high places in your industry and are frequently referred to as an expert in your field, you are certain to attract favorable attention in your company. CEO probably will ask himself if you are so highly regarded by other leaders in the same line of business, shouldn't he move you along faster and perhaps even groom you as his successor. Taking the industry guru road to the top is best described as the three D approach—desirable, difficult, and dangerous.

Industry guru is a highly desirable role because it can lead to your becoming Number One, provide you lots of personal pleasure and earn you much prestige while you are in the process of moving to the top. But the difficulties and dangers associated with becoming an industry guru should be evaluated very thoroughly before deciding to take this route.

You earn the distinction of recognized industry guru by attending many meetings of and holding important offices in industry trade associations; appearing frequently as a speaker at meetings of other industries; writing articles (or having them ghosted for you) for the trade press, business publications, and general interest magazines; and serving as a regional or even national spokesperson for your industry or as a disseminator of the business point of view. In that list of functions lie the reasons why attaining the role of industry guru is both difficult and dangerous.

Being known as an industry guru puts you on center stage, the private domain of Peerless Leader. If there are important industry meetings to attend, he will do the attending. If there are important offices to hold, he will do the holding. If there are articles to be written, he will have his stable of ghosts turn out a dazzling bunch of prose. If there are words of wisdom to be imparted to the unenlightened, or opinions to be expressed, Number One will do the imparting or expressing.

A few, very few, CEOs avoid public attention and designate someone a level or two below them to represent the company in the public arena. The real source of their humility may be recognition of their limitations.

Number Ones, by virtue of their exceptional abilities and high degree of competence, are usually quite eager to demonstrate their superior gifts in public, whether or not the talents which placed them on the pedestal of power be real or imagined. To seek to become an industry guru while you are working for one is to waste your time and imperil your future—in fact, your present.

Those who reach the top spot by accident of birth seem to fall into two categories, both extreme. The vast majority are determined to demonstrate to all that they are no accident, but in truth possess a veritable surfeit of skills and cunning which would have made them brilliant successes even if their parents had been tenant farmers. If your leader is the "I have something to prove" type, accept the fact that he, and he alone, will be the industry guru in your company.

You have some hope if your CEO is the seldom encountered other type of born leader—one who is fully aware of why he is where he is, accepts his limitations, and is completely free of the need to impress anyone. He feels no compulsion to attend meetings, hold office, give talks, write articles, or grant interviews. He prefers to do what he enjoys doing. The possibility always exists that he is stupid. So what? At least he recognizes his lack of brainpower.

Best of all from your standpoint, he won't be second-guessing what you do, say, or write in your capacity as industry guru. Not only will he not be interested in what you do, say, or write, he won't bother to watch what you do, listen to your speeches, or read your writings. That he may not understand what you are doing, talking, and writing about is unimportant.

But never accept the role of personal spokesperson for a not too bright leader. As John Foster Dulles put it, "No point in being at the end of a transmission line if the power house itself [is] not functioning."

For these and other reasons it is exceedingly difficult to become an industry guru. It is, however, much easier to become a semi-guru. A semi-guru is expert in a particular specialty and adequately knowledgeable about industry and general business affairs. A semi-guru must also be capable of attracting some attention from industry leaders, trade and business press, and the general media without incurring Exalted One's wrath. A successful semi-guru must at all times give the appearance of complementing, rather than competing with, leader's industry guru activities.

A semi-guru should never be confused with a quasi-guru, one whose all-knowingness is limited strictly to his specialty. If you know practically everything there is to know about your own field, but have little interest in or awareness of what is going on in other segments of your industry, do not succumb to any opportunities or temptations to become a quasi-guru. Better not to try to be a guru than to end up a quasi.

Quasi-gurus are regarded as tunnel-trained, in touch only with their special interest and oblivious to everything else going on in the world. After speaking at a meeting, quasi-gurus are expected to leave immediately so as not to waste their time listening to others they do not understand. The best a quasi-guru can hope for is to end up as a department head.

If you can handle the role of semi-guru and feel comfortable playing it, take the part, but first make sure you perform in the shadow of CEO and with his enthusiastic endorsement. Quoting him as your source is a good ploy, but don't overdo it. You don't want everyone in your industry to regard you as a mere puppet. Anytime your quote of him is picked up by the press make sure he sees the article. Your hope is that he will become so impressed with your work as semi-guru that, as he begins to wind down his industry activities, he will wind you up to take part in more of them.

Thick skin and fast mind are required of a guru, full or semi. Each time a guru speaks in public or puts words in print, the possibility exists of making misstatements or being too honest, either of which can be quite embarrassing. Your thick skin takes care of you.

But no company appreciates being embarrassed or suffers lightly the fool responsible for the embarrassment. Here's where your fast mind comes into play. Not only must you deny what someone said you said, or claim that you were egregiously misquoted, you must perform this act so convincingly that Leader turns his wrath from you to the dirty bastard who lied or misquoted you. Keep on guruing, but make sure your feet are on the ground rather than in your mouth.

Your high profile produced by your guruing will make you a constant target of your rivals. They will examine microscopically your every word. Federal cases will be made out of suspected errors or misstatements. Watch out for their booby traps.

Obviously, then, the role of guru, full or semi, is only for the few who are poised, tough, tricky, smart, prepossessing, and sophisticated. Having most of these qualities won't be enough to play the role of guru or semi. You must have all of them in abundant supply.

Community service. Call it what you will—noblesse oblige; "To those who much is given, much is required"; or some other high-sounding phrase such as "corporate responsibility." By any term, community service is an absolute necessity for anyone aspiring to a top spot. Playing the role of community leader in a manner which attracts favorable attention can lead to your being selected for a top spot in either your present company or another one.

First you must understand what community service is and what it isn't. It is being associated with civic and charitable causes which attract the upper crust of the community. It is always wearing a white hat and opposing vigorously all black hats. It is concerned with bringing culture to the natives. It means taking the lead in raising money for worthy causes, or those causes deemed worthy by the establishment. It requires attending fund raising events which are formal affairs held at "The Country Club" or another exclusive place where the high society folks hobnob.

Community service does not involve belonging to so-called service or luncheon clubs. It is not concerned with actually soliciting funds by knocking on doors. It is not being president of your college alumni association. These and similar mundane roles in community affairs are for the lower echelon.

Genuine, honest-to-God community service requires playing a leading role in raising funds for charitable and cultural organizations. Being a widely publicized big booster of the arts is especially fashionable. Engaging in such activity is certain to put your name and perhaps your photo in the local paper. You may even be interviewed on TV. If you make the tube, make sure you appear charming, cultured, and urbane, one having a profound interest in the welfare of the community as defined by the establishment of the community.

Never become involved in radical causes or any activities which might reflect unfavorably on any business, such as fund drives to help people pay light and heat bills. The utilities and oil companies are subjected to enough abuse without your adding to their woes.

Number One's blessing on your community service activities is required for them to be useful to you in getting a higher position. Both you and your spouse must exercise great caution to ensure that your efforts to make your city a more livable one do not upstage Mr. and Mrs. CEO in their pursuit of this same noble end.

CHAPTER 18

SETTLE FOR A SINECURE IF YOU MUST

Recognize that the longer you are in one job, the finer the filter you must pass through to be selected for a better role. When you are passed over for a better position several times or someone is brought in from the outside and placed over you, it's decision time. First, reconcile yourself to the reality that you are not going to become CEO or even a top executive. Acceptance won't come easily.

"How in the hell can those bastards upstairs be so stupid as to overlook the most qualified in the place?" you'll ask yourself.

Eventually, and the sooner the better for you, reality will shake you out of your dream world. You will come to recognize that you must determine whether you are going to move to another company with the hope of becoming a leading light there, or stay where you are, forever doomed to dream of what might have been.

Do not deprecate or doubt your ability. Accept the fact that there are more consummate role players in the business world than there are top spots, and that the law of supply and demand applies here. Remember, too, that the powers that be are frequently wrong in their judgments and pick the wrong people. Be cool. Take your time. Make your decision as dispassionately as possible, basing it solely on what you think is best for you and your family without the slightest regard for how you think your decision will affect the company. Although it is truly horrible to contemplate, the sad fact is that the company will get along as well without you as it did with you.

Before making your final decision on going or staying, understand that even though you are not going to end up at or near the top, you need not be a "lifer" in your present position. A better fate is available to you. Pull back a bit from the day-to-day hassle and think about cushy, semi-prestigious jobs in your firm which offer respectable pay, some perks, and relatively little strain or tension. During your mental search for softies, a number of such positions will occur to you. Then focus primarily on those which appear best suited to your particular strengths. Set your sights on those for which you have a somewhat reasonable chance of being selected. Make sure you give consideration to such assignments as the following, which in most companies are open to women as well as men. That the position is presently held by a man should not deter a woman from trying to obtain a soft touch. Placing a woman in a job long held by men can make a firm appear very "equal opportunish."

MEETING PLANNER

Some shows call this role meeting coordinator. Don't worry about what it is called. A job this cushy smells as sweet by any name.

Exercise one caution before setting your sights on this position. If you are with a large company which conducts a substantial number of meetings a year—six or more—don't get involved. You will be too busy working to enjoy the plush perks provided. Planning one or two meetings a year offers the ideal situation, three are OK, four a bit too much, and five tolerable.

Understand that becoming meeting planner will not be easy. Unless the incumbent is on the verge of receiving a gold watch for long and faithful service and a goodbye kiss on both cheeks, a planner is not about to give up the present plum without a tussle. Chances are, you must get the planner out to get yourself in. Try to avoid any bloodshed in the getting out.

Butter up to the present planner. As the job is still held mostly by men, the planner you are trying to replace is probably a man. Convince him he has far too much to do bearing the awesome responsibility of directing meetings in addition to his other assignments. This will likely be an easy sale. When you offer to assist, make sure he understands you want to lighten his load, not compete with him. (Actually, make sure he *mis*understands your intentions, for not only do you intend to compete with him, you also intend to win.)

All assignments given to you by the planner should be executed promptly. Make sure that everything is done right according to the planner's definition of right. Make little deals into big deals. Cover in detail each aspect of the meeting. A mole hill can be blown into a full-fledged mountain through dedicated effort.

As aspiring meeting planner, plump perks await you. Go with the meeting planner two days before the go-early squad departs, and return two days after the stay-lates leave. If meeting planner doesn't invite you to go with him, tell him your early presence on the scene is essential to ensure that all of your pre-meeting chores are handled as he wants them handled. Planner will be naturally reluctant to expose the sybaritic life he leads in those days, but keep on selling until he buys. When you arrive early, you will learn immediately three important lessons: why planner arrives so early; why role of planner is such a desirable one; why planner will be difficult to depose.

Sales manager of the resort or hotel at which your meeting is being held meets your plane. Your bags are carried to a fancy limo. Friendly chatter and happy banter resound throughout the limo during the trip.

Upon arrival at meeting site, planner is escorted to his room by sales manager. You are taken to your room by an assistant manager or bell hop, more likely a bell hop, but possibly the bell captain.

Your room is very nice and may even include a small parlor. Bottles of popular brands of bourbon and scotch and a basket of fresh fruit decorate the coffee table, complete with a note of welcome, not from the sales manager but the general manager or whatever the head honcho at the hotel is called. You are tasting only a morsel. Planner is being served a seven-course dinner.

When you enter planner's room, you may think you went to the Taj Mahal by mistake. In resorts and fancy hotels there are suites, there are s-u-i-t-e-s, and then there are SS-UU-II-TT-EE-SS. You are now in a SS-UU-II-TT-EE. A spiral staircase leads to the master bedroom with mirrors in the ceiling, perhaps mirrored walls.

In the room there are more flowers than there are at a gangster's funeral. There is enough booze to stock the bar at the 21 Club. Now you are beginning to understand why planner will fight fiercely to keep the font of goodies flowing.

Accept the challenge. Start fighting fiercely, but, of course, covertly. Be an eager beaver throughout the meeting. Work hard and make sure that all the leading players see you laboring wholeheartedly, but quite joyfully. Wearing a happy face throughout the ordeal is an important part of your act. You must demonstrate that you really enjoy what you are doing.

Put your copy of the meeting master plan in a big, black notebook. Carry this big, black book with you at all times, even when you go to the bathroom. Refer to the book frequently, especially when the hotshots are watching you. Be the first to arrive and the last to leave each meeting event.

At all times be subservient to and cooperative with the planner. An air of sweetness and tranquility must prevail throughout the entire meeting. The coup must wait until you return home.

All previously outlined caveats regarding meetings apply now, only more so. But additional strictures are attached to your serving as aspiring meeting planner. Do not walk around with a big wad of money in your pocket. Do not tip excessively. Carriers of big wads of money or big tippers are immediately tarred as being profligate with the company's funds in order to buy special personal attention from the hotel's help. Do not sign for any personal item purchased in a hotel shop. Planner personally checks all hotel bills. His accusing you of being a crook can bring your quest for the role of meeting planner to an abrupt halt.

True to the tradition of making each meeting better than the last one, the planner will conduct a meeting post-mortem shortly after all have returned home. The entire meeting will be replayed to determine what went well and what didn't and to solicit suggestions on how to increase interest in and improve the results of the next one. Be very supportive of the planner throughout the post-mortem. Compliment him as frequently and enthusiastically as you can without coming off as his personal cheerleader.

Do not openly seek the job of meeting planner until your boss compliments you on the good job you did in playing "assistant to" planner. If no such praise is forthcoming, forget about becoming meeting planner. You failed the examination.

If the coveted compliment on your performance at the meeting comes from the boss, put the putsch in place. Begin by thanking the boss for the opportunity to play "assistant to." Follow up with a comment about how much you learned from the meeting. Render the coup de grace with the statement, made in an offhand sort of way, that you have a few ideas for reducing costs of and increasing results from future meetings and wonder if the boss would want you to memo your thoughts. A yes answer tells you to proceed full steam with your cabal. Boss's telling you to memo planner translates into: "You are not going to play the role of meeting planner."

In your memo don't concentrate on criticizing what was done; rather, emphasize what improvements can be expected from dropping some features of the past meeting and adding new ones. The trick is to make "different" appear as "better." When discussing cost savings, give amounts. When you must estimate, err on the high side.

For two reasons you should personally deliver the memo to the boss rather than send it through the office delivery system: boss's secretary may show it to planner or even give him a copy; boss may not read it. Tell the boss you are delivering the memo so that you may answer any questions.

Carefully check reactions while the boss reads the memo to help determine your chances of getting the prize. If you succeed in becoming meeting planner, begin immediately to enjoy the fruits of your labors.

Site selection will be an especially juicy morsel. Always personally visit at least five potential meeting spots before selecting one. At each place you will be treated quite hospitably, royally if your meeting is a large one. You may receive nice gifts, tendered not as bribes but merely as remembrances of your visit. Upon departure you will be assured by the head honcho or sales manager that, regardless of your decision, you and your spouse are always welcome as guests of the hotel, whenever you want to come and for however long you want to stay. This generous gesture stems solely from the strong affection the hotel people have developed for you during your visit, so it is perfectly proper for you to accept. But some unsophisticated members of the cast might misunderstand the real motive, so keep quiet about the offer.

All travel agents within a radius of five hundred miles will love you. Those who do business with you will literally adore you. Tokens of their love and admiration will inundate you at Christmas time.

Always observe a potential speaker in action before making a deal. Even some of those who come highly recommended can be real bombs. Limit your auditions to speakers appearing in exotic spots. Anyone accepting speaking engagements in Detroit, Cleveland, Buffalo, and similar industrial cities may have to take anything offered.

By performing well as meeting planner you can make it your full time occupation. Then you can spend nine months living off the perks—checking potential sites, auditioning speakers, and conferring with travel agents, two months planning meetings, and one month vacationing as the guest of fancy resorts.

All things considered, the position of meeting planner can be quite a desirable consolation prize.

PURCHASING MANAGER

Some companies still call this assignment purchasing agent, but most now use the fancier sounding purchasing manager. Regardless of the title, the job can be rewarding in a number of ways.

Your pay won't be anything to shout about, but adequate for living in reasonable comfort. You won't be regarded as one of the firm's authority figures, but controlling all purchases from pencils and paper clips to automobiles and furniture bestows enough power to cause some, especially those in middle management and below, to kowtow to you. It is highly unlikely your role in purchasing computers will be more than a nominal one, if even that. Only those who dwell in that esoteric world are considered sufficiently competent to select the appropriate electronic wizard. Lay people simply do not understand interface and other abtruse functions of the gadgetry.

Anyone who enjoys people fawning over them should check the possibilities of becoming purchasing manager. Salespeople of everything your company buys, may buy, and will never buy will treat you as if you are the most important, charming, and intelligent person they have ever met. They will roar with laughter at your every witticism. Each will be extremely solicitous of your health and that of your family.

Many salespeople will demonstrate their love and esteem for you in ways beyond mere words. If your company is fairly large, you will probably receive four or five luncheon invitations for each working day, so you can be quite selective in your acceptances. Pick those who dine at the best places and bore the least. Vary your hosts. Being seen frequently with the same one may cause a higher-up to think the peddler has you in a pocket. So will the peddler.

So many delivery trucks will fill your driveway at Christmas time that your neighbors may think you are operating an in-home department, liquor, and grocery store. If your company prohibits accepting any gifts from suppliers or specifies what can and can't be accepted, scrupulously follow the rules—at the office. If a friend sends you a gift at home, that is a matter between you and the giver. But use your head. A fancy TV set, video recorder, refrigerator, automobile, or other expensive item is not a gift . . . it is a bribe. Do not succumb to these or similar temptations. Neither jail nor the unemployment line offers a promising future. Strike the salesperson and the company proffering the bribe from your list of suppliers.

Other lures will be dangled before you. You may be offered expense-paid trips to fancy resorts, the Super Bowl, World Series, Broadway plays, and the like. The more brazen may dangle a trip to Europe for you and your spouse. Tell anyone suggesting such a deal that you are not for sale, then start looking immediately for a new supplier of the product you formerly purchased from the would-be briber. If someone suggests that a cash gift or silent interest in the business is available for a large order involving megabucks, tell the crook to get the hell out of your office.

Some companies allow certain departments to buy what they want from whomever they want to buy it. Protect your power base by stopping this practice. Sell the powers-that-be on the wisdom of having all purchases come through you. Expect resistance from those who have been doing some buying. They won't give up the goodies they have been getting from suppliers without putting up a fight. As you uncover purchases made above the going rate, tell the leading lights about the gouging that has been going on to reinforce the need for a single purchasing source.

Once all purchases are placed under your control, take full advantage of your position to put down those who have been pushing you around. Buy them what you think they should have rather than what they want.

Accept the unalterable fact that some unpleasantries are attached to the role of purchasing manager. Count on spending some of your time, perhaps a lot of it, chasing after bargains for Number One. He'll insist on highest quality at lowest price. He may also ask you to supervise the repair of his broken possessions. Many CEOs have a propensity for breaking mechanical gadgets. They are too nostalgic about the old reliable to replace it with a new model. Besides, repairing is cheaper than replacing. Always make sure that old faithful is working perfectly before giving it back to him.

Leader may also ask you to search for an article he saw in New York, London, San Francisco, Paris, or Tokyo but didn't have time to purchase. Proceeding on the vague description he gave you, you are literally off on a wild goose chase. But chase you must, unremittingly, until you find it or he forgets about it.

Your biggest problem as purchasing manager may stem from pressure exerted on you to buy from companies headed by friends of CEO. Even though he may tell you "Give John an equal opportunity, but don't buy unless he matches or beats the others," make sure he means what he is saying. Before buying from another source because of lower price or higher quality, better run your decision by Exalted One before placing the order. If he says to give the order to John because he is much more active in the community, you now know that he did not mean what he said and that in the future you are to buy from his friends.

If CEO deals directly with supplier friends and tells you "We are going to buy from XYZ" or "We are going to use ABC on this project," all you can do is follow his instructions. But you must understand that if the product bought or service rendered is unsatisfactory, the problem is yours, not his.

Purchasing manager need not be a nonglamorous, bound-to-the-desk role. Applying imaginative approaches and a little salesmanship can make it at least partially glamorous and semi-important. Attend trade shows sponsored by manufacturers of products you buy. Be active in the local purchasing manager's association and try to attend national meetings of the group. Add to your staff even if some of them have to spend most of their workday reading supplier catalogues. After all, who makes what for how much is indeed needed information. Require that everyone ordering any item complete lots of forms. Issue lots of cost analyses. Always look busy and preoccupied.

BUILDING MANAGER

Your company must own a fairly large building for you to achieve even reasonable power and status in this position.

The old bromide "A job is what you make it," applies in spades to the job of building manager. You must work very hard at making it seem important for it to have even a modicum of status. You must appear important at all times. Your hope must be that, in time, your appearing important will equate with actually being important.

Building manager is not a big perk job. You will do little, if any, traveling. Any trade association activity will probably be limited to a local group. You'll receive a few Christmas gifts, but likely nothing more than chunks of cheese or jugs of booze.

Possessing a predilection for nit-picking will be useful to you in making the position of building manager appear more powerful than it really is. You must issue all kinds of tissue, with your edicts covering everything from prohibiting the consumption of food on the premises to when the blinds or drapes are to be open or closed.

As Phi Beta Kappas are not inclined to select building maintenance as a career, your associates probably will not be heavily engrossed in intellectual pursuits. If being exposed to hearing "he don't," "between you and I," and other desecrations of the sacred language irritates you, don't seek the job of building manager.

Use your position to wield power and command respect. Assign prime parking places (those not already appropriated by leading lights) to your friends and undesirable ones to your foes. In designing floor plans for various departments, shaft noncooperators, providing such noncooperators are not too high in the pecking order. Flood the editor of the in-house publication with rules and regulations of the building and insist that they be published. Emphasize cost cutting so the hotshots will be properly impressed.

Maintaining a high profile in the building manager's position will strengthen your power base, but will also create problems for you. Number One will call you whenever he has a maintenance problem—at his home as well as his office. Mrs. Number One may summon you when a faucet leaks or when the driveway is covered with snow. Assign your best people to minister to the wants and needs of Mr. and Mrs. CEO, but always go with them and do all of the talking: Maintenance people usually say what they think.

Should you decide to seek the role of building manager, do so in awareness and acceptance of the fact that no bigger jobs are going to be offered to you. But, at the very least, you can give yourself a fancy office in a prime location.

SUPER-SECRET ASSIGNMENT

If you are with a large publicly held company or one in which CEO and other leading lights own substantial amounts of the company's stock but not enough to control, you can try out for one of the most unusual positions available—official preventer of takeover attempts. Unusual may be a considerable understatement.

You will maintain the lowest profile in the place. Probably your title will be completely unrelated to your actual responsibilities. Your pay will be modest, your perks a bit on the meager side, but you will have more access to and receive more attention from Number One than anyone else in the company.

As the one in charge of preventing takeovers, you are to Exalted One what the Strategic Air Command is to the United States—assurance, real or imagined, that if an enemy strikes, the defense plan will quickly annihilate the aggressor. Without such a defense plan, CEOs of all stockholder-owned companies, except a very few huge ones, would never sleep a wink. They suffer from takeover terror, a malady curable only by outright ownership of fifty-one percent of the stock. As effecting that remedy is usually impossible, the disease is practically incurable, so they seek remission through an impregnable defense plan.

Peerless leaders victimized by takeover terror are afflicted by frequently recurring nightmares in which they see the swank that goes with their rank summarily appropriated—strangers flying in their jets, using their telephones in their limos, sitting in their chairs at board meetings, and horror of horrors, cutting up the salary and bonus pie. Palms become quite sweaty while reading about the latest takeover battle. Acid fills a victim's stomach each time the trading volume of the company' stock soars to an unusually high level. The heart beats quite irregularly when the head of a large firm calls seeking a luncheon date "to chat about something of mutual interest." If the caller has taken over one or more companies, peptic ulcers sprout immediately. The torment is unending.

No wonder, then, that a CEO afflicted with this terrible disease insists that impenetrable walls be built around his empire to keep out corporate confreres he refers to affectionately as "God damn raider bastards." Takeover prevention is the one area completely immune from cost-cutting measures. Damn the expense. Protect the fiefdom.

You will not only be allowed, but in fact encouraged by CEO to engage the services of outside experts—proxy solicitors, investment bankers, a public relations firm, a bevy of lawyers—to help you in developing a fail-safe defense plan. The final product will cover each detail of proper defense for each conceivable contingency. The plan will become the most secret document in your company. You will be responsible for maintaining the strict secrecy of all documents related to defense against takeovers and destroying them upon command.

You will monitor closely all transactions in the company's stock and all requests for information on the financial condition of the firm. Both functions provide you an excellent opportunity to puff your part by enabling you to keep Leader in a state of constant concern through manufacturing lots of crises. Always assume the worst when reporting unusual stock trades and inquiries from other companies. CEO will become convinced there are would-be raiders hiding under every desk in the office. Your importance to him is directly related to his level of paranoia.

Soon the leading lights will notice your close ties to Number One and begin showing you more respect. Even though he has designated you as one of his strategic thinkers, a very high honor, the other executives will never be able to accept you as an equal. Most of them don't suffer from takeover terror, at least to the degree CEO does. Some may secretly welcome a takeover, believing that a more enlightened ownership would recognize they should be Number One.

All trips taken and expense reports filed by a takeover fighter are approved without question. You are protecting stockholders from being violated by unscrupulous raiders. Understand, of course, that management's only concern about takeovers, known on Wall Street as non-negotiated mergers, is "acting in the best interests of stockholders." That phrase should, in fact, be given as the reason for each type of "shark repellent" you develop in executing your duties of takeover fighting.

WARNING! Consider the assignment of takeover fighter only if the company has at least a 70–30 chance of winning a takeover fight. Should your firm be swallowed up by a raider, a takeover fighter will certainly be among the first, perhaps the first, to be fired. Sorry, takeover fighter isn't high enough on the totem pole to merit being awarded a work contract, known officially as a "golden parachute."

TOKEN WOMAN

Yes, sad to say, such positions still exist. Although such a role is not for women "goers," it surely can be a lot better than a dead end, routine job. Most token women roles provide prestige, good pay, and attractive perks. Only the lack of any real power keeps it from qualifying as a legitimate top spot.

Official titles of token women vary all over the lot. So do their duties. Any woman seeking the role should sell hard on not having "women" or "women's" in her title. Insist on having your duties include contact with men as well as women.

One of your responsibilities may be representing your company at civic functions. Don't just attend and forget about it. Memo your boss on each event attended. Remember, a key aspect of role playing is disguising activity as usefulness.

Very likely you will maintain a high profile in the firm. After all, your true purpose is to be on display when it is to the company's advantage to display you. Chances are good your photo will appear in a prominent place in the annual report to show the world just how far-thinking your firm is. Always keep in mind that appearance is very important to a token woman. Never buy the line "We want these photos to depict actual conditions, so we are doing candids." Simply refuse to pose for photos taken by a shutter clicker. Insist on having a top-flight portrait studio take the shots. If you aren't satisfied with the proofs, insist on a retake.

You may also be asked to write a section of the annual report covering your duties, at least your alleged ones. Here again, try not to have your comments limited to women, but settle for that if you must. Even that kind of exposure is better than none. And don't accept anything the ghost writer gives you. Your name, not ghost's, appears on the byline. If need be, hire an outside writer to give you a piece of deathless prose.

Attending industry meetings is another of your possible functions. Before going, become familiar with the topics which are going to be discussed and bone up on each one so that you can talk about them in an intelligent and impressive way. Who can tell? Some other CEO may be so impressed with you that he hires you for a job in his company which does offer some real power. The more you act like you are presently a top executive in your company, the more likely the pick-off play will occur.

Token woman is not an all peaches-and-cream assignment. There will be some frustrating moments, some very intense. When anyone playing token woman becomes almost overwhelmed by lack of real power and is tempted to say "stuff it," she should look around and observe the jobs being performed by other women. After such a reappraisal she will surely say to herself: "This may not be real, but it sure beats pounding a typewriter."

Accepting becoming part of the backstage crew. It is highly unlikely that CEO would be so lacking in style and grace to give official notice to subordinates that, unlike college professors, they do not earn tenure. Nor would he be so crass as to suggest to those promoted to bigger jobs that they save the salary increase resulting from their promotion so their life styles won't crumble if they do not perform their new assignments satisfactorily. To publish such a statement would infer that the leading lights don't know what they are doing when they promote people.

Nevertheless, it is a fact of business life that anyone who rises risks falling, so an aspiring executive should understand that the day may come when the choice is a lesser job or none at all. There won't be advance warning. Downgrading an executive is discussed only behind closed doors and in hushed tones.

If Number One summons you to his office and starts telling you about an operation he thinks has been neglected far too long, become suspicious. If he tells you that after an intensive search you have been selected to head this suddenly important function, recognize that you are being removed from the executive ranks. You don't have to accept the move, but you do owe it to yourself to understand what is really happening to you. Role players succeed by fooling others, not themselves.

CEOs embellished explanation of what is happening will not add to your understanding. He will describe your new assignment in grandiose terms to assuage your hurt and hyper your ego.

Your head will be full of questions: "Why am I being kicked out of my present job?"; "What about my salary?"; "Do I still get a bonus?"; "What is my title?" Keep your mouth shut. Your heart is full of anger. Leader's evasive answers may cause you to become violent.

Although you should understand what is really happening to you, continue to profess to be a faithful follower. Pledge to fill the recently recognized void so effectively that soon the operation will be one of the most important and productive in the company. Smile and beg your leave.

As Exalted One leans back in his fancy chair, ruminating on yet another masterful performance, close your office door and begin thinking as objectively as you can under present, trying circumstances. Tell no one about your fall.

In deciding to stay or stuff, keep in mind that your best opportunity to win a top position in another company is while you have at least a somewhat important job in your present one. The right time to go is before you become a goner. You would be stupid to tell the personnel director of another company about your being relegated to obscurity. CEO certainly won't tell. He will rejoice at your leaving and at being freed from the burden of your dead weight.

Should you decide to take your new assignment, you must accept the fact that CEO is determined to keep you in the background. You will be severely tempted to deceive yourself into believing your activities are actually meaningful and that you remain an important member of the executive team. Your ego will be as desperate for accolades and recognition as the damned in hell are for reviews of their cases. Save yourself further frustration. Somehow convince yourself that your importance is over . . . forever.

No rewards are available to you for attempting to regain high standing, but there are risks for not facing facts. Your behavior may become so boorish that CEO may call up the courage to fire you. Fired deposed executives are not in big demand. So if your pay and bonuses keep flowing in large amounts, swallow your pride, keep your mouth shut, and live well.

CHAPTER 19

MOVE ON IF YOU DON'T MOVE UP

Every six months pause and compare your progress with that of your rivals. If rivals appear to be passing you up, attempt to determine why. You may discover that you need to sharpen your role-playing skills in order to quicken your pace of progress.

After three or four years of playing an executive role it should become clear to you whether you have a chance of becoming CEO or a leading light. If you determine that you are not going where you want to go in the company and won't settle for a sinecure, don't blame yourself for your fate or doubt that the top is your rightful place. Keep alive your dream of reaching the top. Your present show isn't the only worthwhile one. Surely somewhere there is one which will recognize and reward someone with your executive ability. Find it!

Use your contacts. Through your travels, speaking appearances, and community service, you have by now developed friendships, at least acquaintanceships, with quite a number of important people, including some CEOs. Milk each contact for all it is worth. Send those who are truly powerful Christmas or Season's Greeting cards with a personal note expressing best wishes and letting them know you and yours are getting along very well.

Invite a head hunter friend to lunch. Play it cool, don't give the slightest indication you are looking for a new connection. Such an admission is strictly a no-no. Head hunters always seek the person, never vice versa. But there is no rule prohibiting your telling head hunter how well you are doing, ticking off a few of your spectacular achievements, and citing the bright future ahead of you in your present company.

A sure way to get a head hunter's undivided attention is to make a casual comment that you are growing weary of receiving offers from other firms, as you are completely satisifed with your present position and future prospects. Chances are that the head hunter will allow your remark to pass without comment.

As soon as the two of you part, the head hunter will put your name in the ever-present black book with the notation: "Receives lots of offers. Satisifed with present position. Highly regarded by company." Hunter knows that in both good and bad times, there is always a demand for outstanding performers who are making it big at their present firm. Head hunter is not about to let a competitor pick up the fat fee involved in placing you in an executive suite.

Collect IOUs from important people you meet along the way. Be alert to opportunities to do favors for your hotshot friends, such as getting them hard-to-find tickets for fashionable events, finagling a hotel reservation, or taking them to your club. Do not consider buying a drink for a leading player in another company as an IOU; everyone in business buys a drink for anyone else in business.

Don't be too anxious. Of utmost importance in catching on with another company is allowing the job to seek you, rather than your seeking the job. Do not contact any employment agencies. Use head hunters only in the manner previously described in this chapter. Either answering a want ad or placing a situation wanted ad is unthinkable for an executive.

When you are invited to apply for an important position in another company, resist becoming so carried away by the thought that someone really does want you that you appear too anxious and turn off the decision maker. Nor should you jump at the first offer as long as you have a respectable position in your present company. Throughout the interview act as if you are completely satisfied with your present job and totally committed to your company.

Before each interview, learn as much as you can about the background and personal characteristics of the CEO of the firm you are considering joining. After you have signed on, you may discover that the kind, friendly, and thoughtful man you talked to at your tryout has suddenly transformed into a tyrannical, stupid, and feckless fool. Living with a mistake of that magnitude is always difficult and frequently disastrous.

Check carefully the ages and length of service of all the top executives. If most are up in years and long in service, keep looking. Gerontocracies may work well in Sun City, Arizona, but are certainly not for role players.

Use a new act. Obtaining a top spot in another company requires putting on an act quite different from the one you used to be promoted to or hired as a junior executive of your present company. Now you are polished, slick, suave, and charming. Use all of your finely honed role-playing skills. Tell what it takes to get you, rather than ask what is offered.

Limit your discussions to here and now. Futures (the personnel director probably will call them futurities) are uninteresting to you at this point in your career. You have served your time in the background. Now you are seeking lots of time in the limelight.

Your new salary and bonus arrangement must be a minimum of twenty-five percent more than your present one. If you are offered less than the acceptable minimum increase, do not snicker, sneer, or frown. Rather, break into a slight smile to indicate: "These people must be kidding." Don't dicker—you get at least twenty-five percent more or no deal—period.

Insist that your line of authority be distinctly delineated. Secure an agreement, preferably in writing, on who reports to you and to whom you report. Unless you report directly to CEO, forget this company and look for another. Make an exception if you will be reporting to a Number Two already officially anointed as successor to Number One.

Accept only total authority and responsibility for your operation. Reject outright any proposal to share authority and/or responsibility. Be equally adamant in refusing to accept assurances that the other one will be eased out but more time is needed to work out the details. Make them put in writing not only that the purge will occur, but also a stated deadline for the guillotine job. Insist that the agreement guarantees that in the interim the bastard will stay out of your way.

Reject any position not providing the amount of travel with which you are comfortable. Apply the same rule to opportunities offered for speaking to company or outside audiences.

Although you can't, or at least shouldn't, ask direct questions about your expense account policy to determine its liberality or lack thereof, this subject is so important to your future that you must do some probing. At the very least, learn if expenses are reimbursed on an incurred or on a per diem allowance basis. Per diem payment gives you another good reason to exit quickly.

Use care in dangling. Being able to accept or reject an unsolicited offer purely on its merits is the best possible situation. Dangling an offer of a position in another company as a means of getting a better job in your present one is less desirable, and somewhat dangerous, but sometimes necessary.

Never dangle unless your new job and company are at least as good as your present ones. Be sure the management of the new firm is as competent as that of the old one. But never dangle unless you are really prepared to leave.

Once you are convinced that dangling is your best route to the top or at least to a hell of a lot better job than you presently have, follow the instructions given in this chapter for inducing other companies to come after you. As would-be danglers seem to be naturally impatient, you may decide to seek a new position on your own if another company doesn't come after you within what you consider a reasonable time after you have decided to dangle.

Exercise great caution in your search for an offer to dangle. Ignore assurances such as "All inquiries are handled confidentially." Assume the role of dangler fully aware that word of your contemplated treason can easily leak to some top executives in your present company. Accept the fact that premature disclosure of your attempted desertion involves a minimum penalty of being removed from the list of promotables.

At interviews you initiated, follow the old "just testing the market" line. Only a totally unreasonable person can quarrel the soundness of the logic of "I will never know if I can improve my position until I find out for myself. Although I am progressing very nicely and am quite satisfied, one should always be alert to greater opportunities." If the personnel director doesn't buy that, you wouldn't want to be associated with the narrow-minded jerk under any circumstances.

Praise, never denigrate, your current CEO, immediate boss, company, and future opportunities. No company wants a disgruntled troublemaker on board, but especially a would-be executive. Don't tip off the personnel director that your real motive is to leave with an offer you can dangle. Give the impression you are selecting them, but not as forcefully as you would had the company sought you. Play it down the middle, being neither too anxious nor too nonchalant.

If the offer received is one you can live with, accept it, otherwise say no. Remember, if your dangle malfunctions, you will have to live with your new job. Offering to give your answer after you have discussed the proposition with your boss at your present company is not merely unthinkable, it is downright stupid. Your prospective new company will immediately recognize you as a dangler and will back off, perhaps even withdraw the offer. Your present firm will recognize your act (dangling is an old play) and bid you bye-bye. Dangle only set-in-concrete offers.

Give the impression to your present company that your new one came after you. If you are confronted with facts which prove the opposite is true, fall back on the "just testing the market" line. When telling your present company "So long, it's been nice to know you," be profuse in your thanks to and praise of superiors, peers, and the firm. Then sit and wait.

Should your dangle produce the desired counter-offer, don't jump at it. Make your first response a flat no. If the new offer includes more power, pay, perks, and status than the other company's deal, bend a bit. Tell the maker of the counter-offer that, out of courtesy to people you respect and admire so much, you will seriously consider the counter-offer. Promise to give your final decision within two days. After two days, but never before, lest you appear too anxious, accept the counter-offer. Tell them that after deep soul searching you have concluded that the company and the people mean so much to you that you felt you had to stay. Make no mention of the sweetening of the pot. Act as if that should have been done long ago. If the counter offer isn't materially better than the deal you have cut with the new company, say no and mean it.

Leave before you become desperate. Once you are convinced you are stymied forever in your present job and believe your skills deserve better than your being typecast as a lifer in a middle or low position, start looking for another company. Regardless of how quickly you want out, use caution in your looking. You don't need to be as cautious as you would if you were going to dangle, but still exercise a fair amount of discretion. Use the "just testing the market" line, not so much to protect your present position as to impress the personnel director at the company you are trying to sell. Do not broadside your resume. Appearing shopworn makes you not just undesirable, but unacceptable.

Never admit you are convinced you have been indelibly marked as a lifer at your current company, not even to your closest confidant. Confidants exist only in mythology. Once your facade of comer chips, your price tag gets marked down sharply.

After you succeed in hooking on with a new company, puff your new position to your superiors and peers at the firm you are about to leave. Follow the line that is one of those truly once-in-a-lifetime deals, one that anyone of sound mind couldn't refuse.

Saying goodbye. In your "exit interview," tell your boss how truly difficult it was to decide to leave all your dear friends and cut your ties to this wonderful company. Putting on paper your love and affection for the firm and all associates makes for an even cleaner cut.

Keep in mind that the company you are about to leave is run by top-flight role players. They will carry on the charade of mutual admiration until you depart. At the least you will be given a farewell luncheon. Or you may be honored at a reception or perhaps even with a dinner party at a fancy restaurant.

It is unlikely CEO will attend and preside, but he may make a brief appearance. Your boss or perhaps your boss's boss will perform as master of ceremonies. Probably your spouse will be invited.

The master of ceremonies recites your outstanding accomplishments during your career, your sterling personal qualities, and the great respect all have for you. The panegyric will also probably include reference to your outstanding family and how much all of you are going to be missed. Some of your peers may also express love and esteem for you.

Then comes the bearing of gifts. There may be one or two humorous ones, but at least one will be of value and substance. Your spouse most likely will also be presented "a permanent reminder of our love and respect for you." You may also receive a card signed by all your associates.

Now it's your turn to express your sorrow at leaving such wonderful people and an outstanding organization. Display no humor, you are involved in a heartrending experience. As you declaim how rewarding and enriching your time with the company has been for you and your family and how much the friendship of those who are soon to become former associates means to you, let your voice tremble a bit and flick a tear from your eye (at least act as if you are). Assure everyone that the gifts given you will always be treasured, more for their meaning than their value.

All your associates present think you are a pushy, arrogant, overrated, self-centered fake who has been a drag for a long time. They wonder just how in the hell you fooled your new company. They are glad to see you gone.

You are delighted to be leaving these stodgy fussbudgets and their inept, antediluvian methods of management. You are filled with gratitude that at last you will be working for a "with it" company which will appreciate your efforts. Don't worry about the sham of it all. Understand what seasoned role players understand . . . it is part, an integral part, of American business to hug and kiss upon leaving for a new company as you begin to start the role-playing process all over again.

CHAPTER 20

PERSIST IN YOUR ROLE PLAYING

While you are in the process of developing into a top-flight role player, you may be plagued by doubts about the efficacy and perhaps even the ethics of role playing. You may think of your conduct as entirely superficial. Some may accuse you of possessing this totally undesirable characteristic.

Chances are that during your learning period you will be exposed to books, articles, and seminars on "the evils of specious behavior" and the "ecstasy derived from following the Puritan ethic of giving an honest day's work for a day's pay." You will be told that plotters, impression-makers, and reaction-checkers are suffering from "leprosy of the mind which slowly but inevitably eats away thought processes." You will be assured that virtue is indeed its own reward, that if you give your all to your work, undoubtedly your rewards will surpass your expectations.

Feelings of guilt may creep in from time to time, too. "Maybe I shouldn't have shown up John as much as I did";

"Although I succeeded in cutting Mary off at the pass, it was rather rude of me to interrupt her so often and get her off the track"; "That memo I wrote which drew rave comments from the Big Boss actually said nothing at all"; "That audience responded as if I actually meant what I said."

You may get caught in your act and have to move on to a new company. Don't blame the role-playing art for that mishap—only your lack of skill in practicing it.

Never allow doubts or guilt to cause you to forswear role playing. As you consider your future course of action in the company, think about what you are really doing when you role play.

You are employing the same techniques used by the vast majority of top business leaders (except those who inherited their roles) to make it to the top. You are actually putting your assets in the spotlight and keeping your liabilities closeted.

Don't let the moralizers grind you down. You are also working very hard. But unlike the lifers, you are working very smart, too. Your only basis for judging these do-gooders is on the merits of what they write and say. You don't know what they actually do. If you are not already aware that some moralizers are among the greatest role players in the world, you are now so informed.

Role players need not be dishonest, but they must not be stupid or gullible. Role playing merely consists of following the same rules of the game that the winners follow. It is also the fun way to try to make it to the top. There is something naturally exhilarating about using your wits as well as your skills to get where you want to go.

And, finally, what is so wrong or immoral about trying to be impressive? Lots of occupants of mediocre positions are efficient. Some are even effective. But they haven't gotten anywhere and they are not going anywhere because they are not impressive. Some people may be enthralled by the qualities possessed by losers, but don't you be one of them.

Your reexamination of the true merits of role playing should convince you not only to continue to play a role, but also to be the very best role player you can be. But never become so enthusiastic about the art that you publicly endorse it. In fact, referring to someone as "just a role player, all form and no substance," is about the most effective put-down one can render.

You should talk a lot about the importance of cooperative effort but actually involve yourself in the practice only when it appears likely you will benefit directly from it. You should use others to help pull you to the top. Once you get there you should espouse spotting and nurturing young talent, but don't get involved personally, for in the process of trying to pull someone up you might get pulled down. The difference between your public utterances and private practices can be a top spot and a rut.

In deciding whether to keep on role playing or to go straight, knowledge of calculus is not required to come up with the right answer. Figure it out this way: your rivals are role players. Your choice is either being a victor *with* it or becoming a victim *of* it. Persist in your role playing.

INDEX